Contents

Foreword by the Secretary of State

This White Paper spells out what the Government proposes to do to modernise social services, in line with our proposals for the NHS and for improving public health and reducing health inequalities which we have already published. We are determined to have a system of health and social care which is convenient to use, can respond quickly to emergencies and provides top quality services. We haven't got that at present. Despite the efforts of a lot of very dedicated staff many services are not provided sufficiently conveniently, promptly or to a good enough standard.

Yet these services are very important. They range from meals on wheels for elderly people, to help at home for people suffering from mental or physical ill health, to placing in residential care children who may be in danger at home. The help comes in many forms, at home, in day centres or by way of residential or nursing home care. It is provided by local councils and by voluntary and private organisations.

One big trouble social services have suffered from is that up to now no Government has spelled out exactly what people can expect or what the staff are expected to do. Nor have any clear standards of performance been laid down. This Government is to change all that.

We propose to set new standards of performance and will publish annual reports on all councils' performance. We will introduce a Commission for Care Standards for each region to regulate residential and domiciliary care, whoever provides it. We will strengthen the role of the Social Services Inspectorate, and the Joint Reviews that they do with the Audit Commission, with tough new powers for the Secretary of State to step in when standards are not met. We will raise professional and training standards through a General Social Care Council whose job will be to ensure the proper regulation and training of social services staff.

Doing things properly doesn't necessarily cost more than doing things badly. Sometimes it can even be cheaper. But we recognise that extra funds are required and over the next three years nearly £3 billion extra will be found. £1.3 billion will form a Social Services Modernisation Fund to lead the major changes that are necessary across the whole social services programme.

Social services provide vital services to some of the most deprived people in all parts of our country, inner cities, suburbs, small towns and rural areas. Many of the most needy also require help from the health service and other agencies. In future they must work together in partnership for the benefit of local people. And we will change the law to promote such partnership. These and the dozens of other proposals in the White Paper will promote independent and fulfilling lives, improve protections for vulnerable people, and raise standards across the board. They will give us modern and dependable social services to match the modern and dependable NHS we are creating. That's why I am confident they will command the support of users and carers, the staff and everyone else of good will.

The Rt Hon Frank Dobson MP
Secretary of State for Health

What are social services?

Social services provide a wide range of care and support for:

- elderly people, through residential care homes, nursing homes, home carers, meals on wheels, day centres, lunch clubs
- people with physical disabilities or learning disabilities
- people with mental health problems, ranging from support for those with mild mental illness, up to exercising legal powers for compulsory admission to psychiatric hospitals of potentially dangerous people
- people with drug or alcohol abuse problems, and ex-offenders who need help with resettlement
- families, particularly where children have special needs such as a disability
- child protection, including monitoring of children at risk
- children in care, through fostering, accommodation in children's homes and adoption
- young offenders.

They are also responsible for the inspection and registration of care homes and other services, to ensure adequate standards and safeguards for users.

Social services are the responsibility of 150 English local authorities. Those authorities work with the voluntary sector and private social care organisations, as well as with other state agencies, to provide local people with the care they need.

1

Key themes

- *the need for modernisation*
- *the third way for social care*
- *the Social Services Modernisation Fund*

Introduction

towards modern social services

> *'any decent society must make provision for those who need support and are unable to look after themselves'*

1.1 Social services are for all of us. At any one time up to one and a half million people in England rely on their help. And all of us are likely at some point in our lives to need to turn to social services for support, whether on our own behalf or for a family member. Often this will be at a time of personal and family crisis – the onset of mental illness, the birth of a disabled child, a family break-up, a death which leaves someone without the carer they had come to rely on.

1.2 We all depend on good social services to be there at such times of crisis, to help in making the right decisions and working out what needs to be done. And more widely, we all benefit if social services are providing good, effective services to those who need them. Any decent society must make provision for those who need support and are unable to look after themselves. Breakdowns in services for young offenders, homeless people, or people with mental health problems can have damaging consequences for other people as well as the individuals themselves. Factors such as demographic changes, and changes in the patterns of family life, are likely to mean that the need for social services will increase in the coming years. With recent advances in health care, more people, including those with profound disabilities, are able to live longer, and they rely on effective social services to achieve more fulfilling lives.

1.3   Social services, therefore, do not just support a small number of
"social casualties"; they are an important part of the fabric of a
caring society. It is a concern for everyone that social services should
be providing the best possible service.

1.4   That objective is not being met. Despite some excellent services in
many places, and a generally high appreciation of services by users,
social services are often failing to provide the support that people
should expect.

Protection

All too often children and vulnerable adults have been exposed to
neglect and abuse by the very people who were supposed to care for
them. There have not been effective safeguards, and the ones that
did exist were frequently ignored. The Utting Report on children's
safeguards highlighted significant failings; and the House of
Commons Health Select Committee recently reinforced those
findings. Recent inspections by the Social Services Inspectorate (SSI)
have found examples where protection systems have failed. This
does not just include instances of abuse but also children identified
as at risk not being monitored by social services. Equally worrying
are cases where people with learning disabilities or elderly people
are neglected or mistreated, or live in conditions which nobody
would want to call their home. Any decent society owes to every
child a safe and secure upbringing, and to every elderly or disabled
man or woman the right to live in dignity, free from fear of abuse.
These duties must be given greater effect in future.

Co-ordination

Sometimes various agencies put more effort into arguing with one
another than into looking after people in need. Frail elderly people
can be sent home from hospital, and do not get the support which
was promised; or they are forced to stay in hospital while agencies
argue about arranging the services they need. Recent Audit
Commission findings have also shown poor coordination between
housing and social services. Everyone deserves to be treated as an
individual, and to have the system geared to their needs, not vice versa.

'it is a concern for everyone that social services should be providing the best possible service'

'lack of clarity of objectives and standards'

Eligibility criteria

Authorities should have clear rules about who can get help – for instance, in what sorts of circumstances someone would get help with dressing or washing at home. These rules (usually known as eligibility criteria) should mean that everyone in that area gets treated fairly. Eligibility criteria should also cover charging issues, so that people can know if they will have to pay for services, and how much.

Inflexibility

Although social services help many people to live fuller and more active lives, they sometimes provide what suits the service rather than what suits the person needing care. Groups with specific needs, such as people from ethnic minorities, can be poorly served. Often services are not planned and provided in a way that would best help service users and carers to get on with their own lives. If this happens it can increase dependency and exclusion instead of alleviating them.

Clarity of role

Up to now, neither users, carers, the public, nor social services staff and managers have had a clear idea which services are or should be provided, or what standards can reasonably be expected. There is no definition of what users can expect, nor any yard-stick for judging how effective or successful social services are. Individuals do not know what services are available, in what circumstances they might get them, or whether they will have to pay. This lack of clarity of objectives and standards means that on the one hand social services cannot be easily held to account, and on the other hand they can get blamed for anything that goes wrong.

Consistency

Social services are a local service, and vary from one part of the country to another in response to differing local needs and circumstances. This is inevitable – an inner city area such as Tower Hamlets will not have the same mix of social services needs as a rural area like Devon, and it would be pointless to try to impose uniform services everywhere. However, there must be national standards so that we can avoid some people not getting the level of quality of service that Parliament has said should be available everywhere. For instance, in some authorities one in five children in care are moved three times or more in one year, while the best authorities manage to keep this down to one in fifty. There is also often inconsistency within one area, with different people getting different services according to what day it is and who they speak to. Eligibility criteria are not clear, and this creates a strong feeling of unfairness. Differences in how charging works from one area to another can also seem unfair.

Inefficiency

An important finding of the Joint Reviews so far is that there is scope for many authorities to get more for what they spend on social services. The costs of services differ substantially from one authority to another, with often a 30 per cent difference in unit costs for the same service between similar authorities in the same part of the country. By running services more efficiently, some councils could save as much as £10 million, which could be used for better services.

> **Joint Reviews**
>
> Joint Reviews of social services are carried out by the Social Services Inspectorate (SSI) and the Audit Commission. They are a new type of review, and combine for the first time the service expertise of the SSI with the Audit Commission's understanding of value for money and effectiveness. They look at the performance of each authority across the whole of its social services responsibilities, and produce a published report. The Joint Reviews cover 20 authorities each year, and have so far published reports on 27 of the 150 councils responsible for social services in England.

1.5 There are various reasons for these and other failings in the system, and the Government must take its share of the responsibility for tackling them. People who work in social services have to deal with some very difficult people and many very difficult circumstances. They often find themselves the target for criticism, and their sense of vocation is often underestimated. The Joint Reviews and SSI inspections show that criticism of the service is justified, but the Government has no wish to add further to the criticism of those who work in social services. We recognise that the law and the central framework within which social services operate is also at fault. They need to be changed so that they help those working in the services rather than hindering them.

1.6 That is why there is an agenda for modernisation which will need action at national as well as local level. The problems cannot be resolved overnight, and will take time and effort to put right. But the Government is determined to tackle the failures it has identified, and intends to undertake a series of reforms that will lead to a radical improvement of social services. This White Paper explains the new approach.

'the Government is determined to tackle the failures'

'our third way for social care moves the focus away from who provides the care, and places it firmly on the quality of services experienced by individuals and their carers and families'

1.7   The proposals in the White Paper look to the future, to the creation of modern social services. The last Government's devotion to privatisation of care provision put dogma before users' interests, and threatened a fragmentation of vital services. But it is also true that the near-monopoly local authority provision that used to be a feature of social care led to a "one size fits all" approach where users were expected to accommodate themselves to the services that existed. Our third way for social care moves the focus away from who provides the care, and places it firmly on the quality of services experienced by, and outcomes achieved for, individuals and their carers and families.

1.8   This third way for social care is based on key principles which should underlie high quality effective services. These principles are at the heart of our modernisation programme set out in this White Paper:

- care should be provided to people in a way that supports their independence and respects their dignity. People should be able to receive the care they need without their life having to be taken over by the social services system

- services should meet each individual's specific needs, pulling together social services, health, housing, education or any others needed. And people should have a say in what services they get and how they are delivered

- care services should be organised, accessed, provided and financed in a fair, open and consistent way in every part of the country

- children who for whatever reason need to be looked after by local authorities should get a decent start in life, with the same opportunities to make a success of their lives as any child. In particular they should be assured of a decent education

- every person – child or adult – should be safeguarded against abuse, neglect or poor treatment whilst receiving care. Where abuse does take place, the system should take firm action to put a stop to it

- people who receive social services should have an assurance that the staff they deal with are sufficiently trained and skilled for the work they are doing. And staff themselves should feel included within a framework which recognises their commitment, assures high quality training standards and oversees standards of practice

'staff themselves should feel included within a framework which recognises their commitment, assures high quality training standards and oversees standards of practice'

- and people should be able to have confidence in their local social services, knowing that they work to clear and acceptable standards, and that if those standards are not met, action can be taken to improve things.

1.9 In this White Paper, the Government commits itself to these principles, and spells out how it intends to deliver the necessary improvements by action at both national and local level. The proposals will support welfare reform and social inclusion by promoting people's independence. They will improve the protection of vulnerable people. And they will raise standards so that everyone can be assured of high quality social services.

Priorities in services for adults and children

1.10 Chapter 2 sets out proposals for change in services for adults, under three priority areas: **promoting independence, improving consistency,** and providing **convenient, user-centred services.** Chapter 3 sets out the priority areas in children's services: **protection, quality of care** and **improving life chances.** Each chapter spells out specific initiatives and actions designed to deliver the necessary improvements.

1.11 The rest of the White Paper sets out our modernisation proposals affecting all social services:

Improving protection

Chapter 4 describes radical changes to the arrangements for protecting people through better regulation of care services. This will strengthen the safeguards for children and vulnerable adults, and establish a tough new independent system for regulation.

Improving standards in the workforce

Chapter 5 sets out proposals for developing and investing in the social care workforce, including the establishment of a General Social Care Council to set practice and ethical standards for staff, give the public greater protection, and give the staff a framework which recognises their commitment and responsibilities.

'social services also need to work in partnership with non-statutory agencies, particularly the voluntary sector and independent care providers'

Improving partnerships

Chapter 6 explains our proposals for better and clearer relationships between social services and other agencies, particularly the NHS; the plans set out will make for integrated care services which give people what they need without delays and red tape. Social services also need to work in partnership with non-statutory agencies, particularly the voluntary sector and independent care providers.

Improving delivery and efficiency

Chapter 7 sets out our new framework for raising standards and ensuring that every local authority provides good quality, best value social services delivering positive outcomes. There will be clearer responsibilities for local government, and a clearer role for central government to take action where standards are not being met. This new performance framework will also ensure that central and local government, working together, deliver the programme of change set out in the White Paper.

1.12 These proposals form part of the Government's wider programme to modernise public services. They tie in closely with a range of other Government initiatives and programmes. They are linked with the radical steps to modernise and strengthen democracy in local government; and the new emphasis on best value and accountability. They also give effect to our commitment to improve inter-agency working between social services and the NHS. And they contribute to our efforts to strengthen family life, reduce social exclusion, tackle youth crime, and reform the welfare state.

'we are also delivering the resources needed for change'

1.13 We are also delivering the resources needed for change. A lot of money is already invested in social services. Spending in England is around £9 billion, and the average social services authority spends £60 million to provide services for local people.

1.14 In the White Paper *Modern Public Services: Investing in Reform*, the Government set out firm three year plans for each area of public spending. The funding for social services will be increased by an annual average of 3.1 per cent above inflation over the next three years, which is a clear signal of the priority the Government is giving to this area. Over this three year period, this amounts to nearly £3 billion extra funding for social services.

1.15 But this is not more money to provide more of the same. It is money for change and modernisation. In return for the extra public investment there must be real improvements in the services given to the public.

1.16 As part of the extra funding, we have therefore created a Social Services Modernisation Fund. This fund will deliver over £1.3 billion of new money targeted at the key areas identified in this White Paper as needing reform.

'in return for the extra public investment there must be real improvements in the services given to the public'

Social Services Modernisation Fund	1999/00	2000/01	2001/02	Total
Promoting independence:partnership grant	£253m	£216m	£178m	£647m
Promoting independence:prevention grant	£20m	£30m	£50m	£100m
Children's services grant	£75m	£120m	£180m	£375m
Mental health grant*	£46.4m	£59.4m	£79.4m	£185.2m
Training support grant*	£3.6m	£7.1m	£9m	£19.7m
Total Modernisation Fund	£398m	£432.5m	£496.4m	£1326.9m

* This represents the <u>extra</u> money in these areas, and is in addition to the current grant levels.

1.17 This funding will be a lever for modernisation throughout all social services activity and spending. Through the Modernisation Fund, and through the wider increases in social services funding, we are providing the resources to match the plans set out in this White Paper.

1.18 Social services are too important to be neglected. This Government will give them the attention they deserve. In partnership with local government and other stakeholders, we will work to ensure that we can all benefit from services fit for the next century.

'in partnership with local government and other stakeholders, we will work to ensure that we all benefit from services fit for the next century'

2

Key themes

- *helping people to live independently*
- *creating fairer, more consistent services for all*
- *making sure services fit individual needs*

Services for adults

independence, consistency, meeting people's needs

Introduction

2.1 Social services for adults are right at the heart of the welfare state. They carry out essential tasks working with a wide range of people – home care services, day centres, residential care schemes, rehabilitation of blind or partially-sighted people, provision of equipment to aid independent living, help to parents with disabilities to carry out their parenting tasks, support for families who have caring responsibilities, work with people with mental health problems, and support to learning disabled people and their families. Over the years, innovative services have been developed in many places to ensure that people get the help they need.

'serious problems remain'

2.2 However the system can be frustrating for anyone who tries to use these services, whether for themselves, or on behalf of friends or relatives. There have been significant changes in adult services since the community care reforms earlier in the decade. But these have concentrated largely on structure and on process, rather than on outcomes. Serious problems remain.

2.3 Decisions about who gets services and who does not are often unclear, and vary from place to place. Eligibility criteria are getting ever tighter and are excluding more and more people who would benefit from help but who do not come into the most dependent categories. Decisions about care can still be service driven, and concentrate on doing things for people according to what is available, rather than tailoring services to the needs of individuals and encouraging those who are helped to do what they can for themselves. Overall, people feel ill-informed about how they should find out about services, what they may be asked to contribute themselves, who will be providing the care, and how they can influence it. This is particularly true for certain groups such as older people from ethnic minorities.

2.4 Social services need direction if they are to serve adults better. In particular, they need to:

- seek to promote people's **independence** while treating them with dignity and respect at all times, and protecting their safety

- provide services **more consistently** across the country

- make the system more **centred on service users** and their families, and as convenient and straightforward as possible for people to use.

The Community Care reforms

In April 1993, social services' responsibilities for people needing long term care expanded significantly. Until that time, people who lived in independent residential or nursing homes were funded through DSS benefits. The Community Care reforms gave social services the responsibility not only to fund this type of care placement (subject, as before, to a means test) but also to carry out an assessment of care needs for the individual concerned, and ensure that the care being given was what that person needed. This focus on individual care management, focused towards helping more people to live in their own homes, was the key change to the system.

'social services need direction if they are to serve adults better'

Promoting independence

The problem

'the guiding principle of adult social services should be that they provide the support needed by someone to make most use of their own capacity and potential'

2.5 We believe that the guiding principle of adult social services should be that they provide the support needed by someone to make most use of their own capacity and potential. All too often, the reverse is true, and they are regarded as services which do things for and to dependent people.

2.6 Because of resource pressures, councils are tending to focus more and more on those most dependent people living in their community. For example, although there has been an increase in the overall level of domiciliary care supporting people in their own homes, that increase has been concentrated on those getting more intensive support, and the number of people receiving lower levels of support has actually dropped (see graph). This means that some people who would benefit from purposeful interventions at a lower level of service, such as the occasional visit from a home help, or over a shorter period, such as training in mobility and daily living skills to help them cope with visual impairment, are not receiving any support. This increases the risk that they in turn become more likely to need much more complicated levels of support as their independence is compromised. That is good neither for the individual nor, ultimately, for the social services, the NHS and the taxpayer.

2.7 People generally want to live in their own homes if they can, and admission to institutional care (whether in hospital or in residential care or nursing homes) can lead to lower self-confidence and a decline in activity. Yet the evidence is that many authorities are setting a financial ceiling on their domiciliary care packages, particularly in services for older people, which can lead to premature admissions to care homes when care at home would have been more suitable.

Trend in provision of domiciliary care, England

— Households receiving 5 hours or more per week

— Households receiving 2 hours or less per week

— Total hours

200
175
150
125
100
75
50
25
0

1992 1993 1994 1995 1996 1997

1992=100

2.8 The number of emergency admissions to hospital of people over 75 has been rising steadily. These admissions, which may well lead to permanent institutionalisation, are avoidable in many cases. People are also being admitted directly to permanent residential or nursing home care on discharge from hospital, even though in a sizeable minority of cases, better rehabilitation or recuperation services could have helped them return to their own homes.

2.9 Once services are being provided, they are often not reviewed. This again contributes to a culture of dependency rather than one of enablement. A great deal of effort is put into initial assessment of care needs, but after that there may be very little review of progress (particularly in residential and nursing home placements) to see whether the user's needs have changed or whether the services are providing the best outcomes. Joint Reviews and SSI inspections of various aspects of adult services in recent years have consistently shown this.

2.10 And finally, the care system does not adequately recognise the enormous contribution that informal carers make to maintaining the independence of people with care needs. Carers are the most important providers of social care: according to the 1995 General Household Survey of Great Britain, they number 5.7 million, with 1.7 million of them providing care for 20 hours or more each week. The Carers (Recognition and Services) Act 1995 provided greater rights for carers, but implementation of it remains patchy. Greater efforts need to be made to recognise and cater for carers' needs.

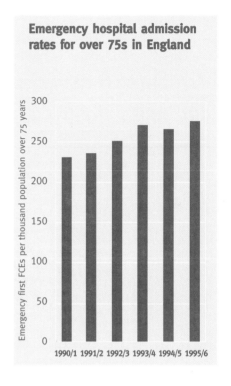

Emergency hospital admission rates for over 75s in England

The 1998 Annual Report of the Joint Reviews notes that in most councils cases are not reviewed unless required by law. The finding is underpinned by users' and carers' experience. Many report that they have not been asked how things are going. Many users and carers have valuable knowledge about services, but many councils are not asking them to share this knowledge.

'social services must aim wherever possible to help people get better, to improve their health and social functioning rather than just "keeping them going"'

Better services for vulnerable people

This initiative was launched in October 1997. It requires all health and local authorities to draw up Joint Investment Plans for developing services to help people get the care they need while avoiding unnecessary hospital or care home admissions. This may include developing specialist rehabilitation services to help people to go back home after a hospital stay, or other initiatives such as dedicated hospital discharge teams.

Action

2.11 The Government will take action to reverse these trends, and to put greater independence at the heart of social services for adults. Our programme of action includes:

- better preventive services and a stronger focus on rehabilitation

- extension of direct payments schemes

- better support for service users who are able to work

- improved review and follow-up to take account of people's changing needs

- improved support for people with mental health problems

- more support for carers.

Prevention and rehabilitation

2.12 We want to put a new emphasis on helping people achieve and maintain independence wherever possible. And when someone does need care, social services must aim wherever possible to help them get better, to improve their health and social functioning rather than just "keeping them going". We have set in train a number of specific measures to ensure that this approach is taken:

- "Promoting Independence" has been identified as one of the priorities for both health and social services in the National Priorities Guidance issued on 30 September this year (see Chapter 7). Authorities are required to implement jointly agreed plans for improving rehabilitation services, as set out in the Better Services for Vulnerable People initiative launched in October 1997

- the Social Services Modernisation Fund will deliver substantial extra funding to help shift the emphasis of service provision to promoting independence. Two new grants will be introduced, totalling nearly £750 million over three years. This grant funding will come with conditions that will ensure that the improvements we want to see are delivered.

Promoting independence: partnership grant

- a new grant, providing nearly £650 million over three years, to foster partnership between health and social services in promoting independence as an objective of adult services

- particular emphasis on improving rehabilitation services; avoiding unnecessary admissions to hospital and other institutional care; improving discharge arrangements; and fostering good joint contingency planning to deal with emergency pressures

- conditions attached to the grant will ensure that local authorities' spending plans are clearly stated in Joint Investment Plans, agreed with the NHS who will set out how their own spending plans contribute to the objectives and complement the new grant.

Promoting independence: prevention grant

- a new grant totalling £100 million over three years, for stimulating the development by local authorities of preventive strategies and effective risk assessment, so as to target some low level support for people most at risk of losing their independence

- encouraging an approach which helps people do things for themselves for as long as possible, in their own home; and helps people of working age take up, remain in or return to work for as long as possible

- authorities will be required by the grant conditions to draw up an action plan (jointly agreed with the NHS) during 1999/2000 setting out their proposals for a preventive strategy.

2.13 We have already seen many excellent examples of joint health and social care services to help promote independence, in response to the extra funding we have made available for winter pressures (see Chapter 6). We are now making this approach a priority in services for all adult client groups, backed up by substantial extra funding. We expect authorities to deliver on this programme, and will monitor progress closely through both the NHS and social services performance frameworks.

Promoting independence: independent living

In Southampton, the Extended Community Care Scheme, or Companion Service, helps older people with dementia who live alone to continue to live safely in their own homes for as long as possible. The service is run by Southampton MIND who provide a companion to befriend and support service users.

Companions provide emotional and social support. But they also give the practical support needed to cope with memory loss, which other services sometimes overlook. For example, confused people can need help understanding what to do with the packages they receive from meals on wheels; they may need someone to collect prescriptions left by a doctor; and they may need accompanying to out-patients so they don't get lost between the ambulance and clinic.

Promoting independence: helping people return home

Outlands is a former home for older people run by City of Plymouth Council. For the last 5 years it has offered 6 weeks rehabilitation to older people leaving the local acute hospital. Between 70% and 80% of people who use this unit have been successfully rehabilitated to their own homes where previously they would have entered long-term residential care. People are able to go home with little if any ongoing support from social services.
5 years on, studies show few have entered long-term care.

Direct payments

2.14 One way to give people greater control over their lives is to give them the money and let them make their own decisions about how their care is delivered. This was made possible for physically disabled people and people with learning disabilities aged under 65, through legislation which came into force last year. Local authorities are now able to offer cash to such people whom they had assessed as eligible for home care, day care or occasional short stays in residential or nursing homes. At the start of this year, around 1,000 people were participating in schemes, in 31 authorities. More authorities are bringing in schemes this year.

2.15 Direct payments are giving service users new freedom and independence in running their own lives and we want more people to benefit from them. We have decided, therefore, to remove the age limit and to make people aged 65 and over eligible for direct payments.

2.16 We will also be seeking to ensure that more authorities are offering this opportunity to service users in their areas. We will be conducting a further survey to see where direct payments schemes are being offered, and to find out from those councils who have no plans for a scheme where the obstacles lie. If the case is strong enough, we will consider making it mandatory for all authorities to operate schemes, to ensure equity of opportunity across the whole country.

2.17 Other changes to direct payments are being considered as part of a review of the scheme to learn lessons from its first year of operation. The review is also looking at how direct payments support independent living by working in conjunction with the other help available, including the Independent Living Fund, a social security fund which provides benefit support on the basis of a social services assessment to very severely disabled people to help them to live independently in the community. When the review is completed early next year, we will consult local authorities and other interested groups on our plans for strengthening and extending the scheme.

Employment

2.18 Employment is one of the most powerful pathways to independence, and our National Priorities Guidance reminds councils of their responsibility to help service users and carers of working age work where possible. Councils are already participating in the Government's New Deal for Disabled People. For example, the innovative schemes for which funding was announced in September 1998 include a project to provide work experience for deaf people in which Lincolnshire social services are involved. Social services also have a role to play in the Single Gateway which we plan to establish for all benefit claimants of working age, including those claiming incapacity benefits. As described in *A New Contract for Welfare: Principles into Practice*, the Gateway will act as a single point of access to welfare, providing personal advisers to help those who can and want to work to gain access to the various services available to them.

Review and follow-up

2.19 People should not be "signed off" once they have had their initial assessment and are receiving services. Good care management should ensure that people's needs are monitored and reviewed. When people are admitted to a care home, or begin to receive care in their own home, case reviews should be carried out within three months. Thereafter, reviews should be carried out at least annually, and should wherever possible be carried out face to face. The frequency of these subsequent reviews will depend on the type of case, and factors such as the uncertain nature of future needs and the complexity and costs of the care package. Councils should be explicit about who is to carry out the review in individual cases – sometimes the provider can play a role here – what it comprises, and how often. Whichever approach is used, it is expected that users and carers will play a full part.

> *'employment is one of the most powerful pathways to independence'*

Promoting independence: a job

In Kensington and Chelsea, social services provide a service, Kensington Recruitment, which works with employers and people with sensory impairment, physical disabilities and learning disabilities to place service users in regular paid employment. Key features of the scheme are:

- one to one support from a professional job consultant
- searching out vacancies
- help in finding the right job
- on site support
- increasing the employability and skills profile of disabled people by making employers aware that disability does not mean inability.

Richmond upon Thames operates a similar scheme where social services operate an employment resource centre for mental health service users.

'people should not be "signed off" once they have had their initial assessment and are receiving services'

2.20 We will set out our expectations on authorities' review activity as part of our Fair Access to Care initiative (described in paragraph 2.36 below); and we will monitor how well authorities are performing as part of the new arrangements for monitoring performance in social services (see Chapter 7).

Improving support for people with mental health problems

2.21 Promoting independence should not, of course, be at the expense of effective and safe services. In particular, in mental health services people have suffered in the past as a result of being left too much to look after themselves. The mental health care in the community system, while helping many people, has failed others. The Government's strategy for developing safe, sound and supportive mental health services, to be published shortly, will aim to promote the health, well being and safety of individuals and the well being and safety of the wider community. The services should be provided to people as close to home as is practicable. More detail on the forthcoming strategy is at paragraph 2.34.

Supporting carers

The London Borough of Merton has established *Care Connect*, a partnership agency which brings together health, social services and the voluntary sector. The project provides a range of support to carers, including:

- drop-in facilities

- a helpline

- access to a wide-range of information via a database linked to the Internet

- respite care in the carer's own home.

Carers in Merton told SSI that they particularly liked respite care being brought to their own home – it was less disruptive than if the person they cared for had to go to residential or day care.

Carers

2.22 We recognise that carers have a wide range of needs – as diverse as the people they care for. Their work is vital and has often gone unrecognised. Support for carers is not just a matter for social services, but for a range of statutory and non-statutory agencies in the housing, employment, education and other fields. The Prime Minister announced on 10 June 1998 the development of a National Carers Strategy, bringing together activity across all Government Departments in support of carers which will take a comprehensive view across all these areas.

2.23 As well as assessing what key needs of carers may have been overlooked and setting out an integrated strategy for future action by Government, the key aims of the Strategy Project include:

- empowering carers so that they have more say about the types of services that they and the person they care for need

- considering how best carers who work can be supported so that they can remain in employment

- considering how the health needs of carers can better be met by the NHS and especially primary care groups

- looking to see how communities can better support carers especially through volunteering

- looking at the specific needs of other groups such as young carers and ethnic minority groups.

2.24 The strategy will seek to highlight existing good practice in a range of areas covering the needs of carers, and build on this. The National Carers Strategy is due to be published early next year.

How will people see the benefits of our changes?

If we succeed in our plans to improve services for adults by promoting independence, the following benefits can be expected:

- people will be offered a service that is designed not just to keep them going, but to improve their capabilities and allow them the maximum possible independence

- when people need social services help, that help will be arranged in a way that lets them do as much as possible for themselves; and allows them wherever possible to live in their own homes

---

All authorities will develop and target a range of preventive services for adults, including respite care; and will agree an action plan in accordance with Department of Health guidance to be issued in the first half of 1999.

National Carers Strategy

The terms of reference for the National Carers Strategy are as follows:

To draw together existing work within Government that impacts on carers; to take account of the emerging findings of the Royal Commission on Long-term Care; to gather examples of best practice in providing help for carers at local level, to assess whether any key needs of carers have been overlooked; to clarify the Government's objectives for carers; to set out an integrated strategy for future action by Government; and to report through the Parliamentary Under-Secretary of State for Health (now Minister of State at the Home Office), to the Prime Minister.

- many more people will be able to have real control over their care support through direct payments schemes

- health and social services will target their support especially on people who are at risk of losing their independence (for instance, elderly people living alone during the winter; people who have just left hospital, or who have a visual impairment, and are finding it hard to cope at home), to make sure that special efforts are made to avoid such people having to be admitted to hospital or a care home

> *We have set a national target to reduce the growth per capita in emergency hospital admissions of people over 75 to 3% by 2002 (against an average of 3.5% in recent years).*

- carers who look after family members, neighbours or friends will be given greater support by social services and other agencies, to allow them to continue to care where that is what they and the person they are caring for want.

> *All authorities will provide carers with the support and services to maintain their health, and with the information they need on the health status and medication of the person they are caring for. As a first step, systems should be in place by April 2000 to identify primary care and social services users who are or who have carers.*

Greater consistency

The problem

2.25 Many people feel that the care system is not fair. There are variations in who gets what services, inconsistencies in what types of provision are available in different parts of the country, and differences in how charging works.

2.26 Eligibility criteria should inform users about what sorts of people with what kinds of need qualify for what types of service. They should also help care managers to carry out effective assessments and then match services to assessed need. However, some eligibility criteria can be so broad or poorly framed that they help neither users nor staff. The ways in which needs are assessed, and the routes through which people get access to services, can vary from authority to authority, or even within a single authority. The 1998 Joint Reviews Annual Report noted: "There appears to be no consistent link between referrals, assessments and services either between councils, or indeed between different services of the same council".

2.27 The result is that someone with long-term care needs might receive high level care in their own home from social services and the NHS in one place, whereas in another they might have to go into residential or nursing home care.

2.28 The social care charging system is also a cause of confusion and concern to many people. There is a national means tested framework for residential and nursing home care charges, which means that everyone is subject to the same system when it comes to care homes. But charges for other services, such as home care, meals on wheels and day centres, are discretionary, with each authority setting its own charges, and its own rules on how those charges work.

'eligibility criteria should inform users about what sorts of people with what kinds of need qualify for what types of service'

2.29 The differences in these discretionary charges can be considerable. The amount that authorities recover in charges – as a percentage of their spending on these services – varies from 4 per cent to 28 per cent. And the charging systems differ enormously from one council to another. For instance, one council might charge a standard hourly rate which everyone – whatever their income – pays, so that the amount paid depends on the amount of care received. Whereas another council might operate a sliding scale of charges according to income, regardless of how much care is received. Taking a random example, someone with a weekly income of £115 and receiving 12 hours of care per week could pay £13 per week in one area, and £48 per week in the other.

'users have always been expected to contribute to the cost of some social care services'

2.30 It has always been the case that the user has been expected to contribute to the cost of some services, particularly residential care, according to an assessment of income. However, there are strong criticisms of the system, both in terms of the fairness of the national charging system for residential care, and in terms of the variation, from one part of the country to another, of the discretionary charges for services in the community.

Action

'there has to be a greater level of consistency and fairness in social care'

2.31 There has to be a greater level of consistency and fairness in social care. The Government's action programme includes:

- taking a greater role nationally in setting objectives and standards for social services

- the introduction of National Service Frameworks, in partnership with the NHS

- a Fair Access to Care initiative

- action to establish greater consistency and fairness in charging.

New objectives and national priorities guidance

2.32 We believe that there should be greater national consistency of objectives and priorities in social services, for both adult and children's services. New national objectives for social services have been drawn up, and they are the foundation of the proposals in this White Paper. The objectives also feed directly into the National Priorities Guidance, a single statement of priorities for both health and social services, which all authorities around the country should follow.

2.33 This stronger direction at national level on the priorities for social services will ensure more consistent, high quality services everywhere in the country. The national objectives and National Priorities Guidance, and how they fit into the new performance monitoring arrangements for social services, are described in more detail in Chapter 7.

National Service Frameworks

2.34 National Service Frameworks (NSFs), announced in the NHS White Paper *The new NHS*, will set national standards and define service models for specific services or care groups. They will achieve greater consistency in the availability and quality of these services, addressing the whole system of care including social care and the wider local authority and their partners. The aim will be to reduce unacceptable variations in care and standards of treatment, based on research evidence on standards, outcomes and cost-effectiveness. One of the first NSFs is on mental health services, and is already being developed (see box).

National Service Framework for mental health services

This is one of the first two NSFs to be developed (the other is for coronary heart disease). Work is currently underway with the establishment of an External Reference Group (ERG) chaired by Professor Graham Thornicroft. The purpose of the NSF is to assist all agencies, statutory and non-statutory, in delivering the Government's strategy for safe, sound and supportive mental health services. The ERG has identified a set of standards to address the quality, comprehensiveness and accessibility of services.

The Government's overall strategy for mental health services, and the emerging findings of the ERG, will be published shortly. The strategy includes plans for substantial extra funding over the next three years, new arrangements for monitoring delivery of mental health services and a commitment to reviewing the Mental Health Act. Social services will be a full and equal partner in delivering this strategy.

2.35 The next National Service Framework to be developed will be on services for older people. This will provide explicit standards and principles for the pattern and level of services required, put in place programmes to support implementation, and establish performance measures. It will be developed, as with all NSFs, with the help of an expert reference group which will engage the full range of views, bringing together health and social care professionals, service users, carers, health and social services managers, partner agencies and other relevant groups.

Fair access to care

'we will develop guidance on Fair Access to Care'

2.36 Alongside the National Service Frameworks for mental health, older people, and other groups or conditions as they are developed, we will also introduce greater consistency in the system for deciding who qualifies for those services. We will develop guidance on Fair Access to Care, which will set out the principles authorities should follow when devising and applying eligibility criteria, including the need for compatibility with NHS continuing care criteria. But it will go wider than eligibility criteria, as these are only part of the story. Key elements will be the need for authorities to show:

- **consistency** in the way that every person's needs are assessed, with fair and transparent procedures and criteria followed in every case

- clear **objectives**, based on the overriding need to promote independence, which should apply at all stages in the process, from initial screening, through to assessment, devising a care package, and monitoring it

- a common understanding of **risk assessment** on which to base decisions about services – what kind of risk someone faces, how serious, its cause, how likely, and so on. Most authorities already assess risk, but in different ways

- **regular reviews.** There needs to be more consistency not only about people accessing services for the first time, but about people already receiving services, to ensure that the services continue to meet objectives.

Charging

2.37 There must be greater transparency and fairness in the contribution that people are asked to make towards their social care. We are committed to finding a way to fund long term care which is fair and affordable for the individual and the taxpayer.

2.38 That is why we set up a Royal Commission in December 1997 to examine the short and long term options for funding long-term care for elderly people, both in their own homes and in other settings. It will be making recommendations early next year. Although it is concentrating on older people, it has been asked to consider the implications of its recommendations for younger people with long-term care needs.

2.39 There is great inconsistency in the discretionary charging system for non-residential care. At the moment, every authority – if it operates a charging system – can develop its own rules for assessing income, which can mean that in one area a certain type of income is taken into account for charges while in another it will be disregarded. The Audit Commission is currently carrying out a major survey of authorities' charging practices, which we expect to show widespread differences in the way that discretionary charges work.

2.40 The Government believes that the scale of variation in the discretionary charging system, including the difference in how income is assessed, is unacceptable. We will consider how to improve the system in the light of both the Royal Commission's report and the Audit Commission survey.

'there must be greater transparency and fairness in the contribution that people are asked to make towards their social care'

'the Government believes that the scale of variation in the discretionary charging system, including the difference in how income is assessed, is unacceptable'

How will people see the benefits of our changes?

Our plans to improve consistency and fairness in social services for adults should produce the following results:

- greater certainty about what services can be counted on in all parts of the country

- greater assurance of quality services everywhere, rather than having to live with second best

- fairer and more transparent rules for deciding who qualifies for services, and greater consistency in applying them around the country

> *By April 2001, every local authority will be working within the Fair Access to Care guidance*

- a fairer system for paying for care, following the outcome of the work of both the Royal Commission and the Audit Commission.

Convenient, user-centred services

The problem

2.41 When the need for social services support or care arises, it is usually a time of great anxiety and fundamental change in the lives of individuals, their partners and families. Decision-making in these circumstances is difficult enough, but it is made even more so by the extraordinary complexity of the system. An array of agencies – NHS, social services, housing, the employment service, benefits – may all have important things to contribute. People need help through the maze. They need clarity about who is offering what, and what the options are. And they need to be provided with services that suit their own particular needs – they should not be asked to fit in willy nilly with whatever services happen to be available. There is no doubt that the situation has improved in recent years, but we are still a long way off having services that are really geared to the individual needs and interests of users.

'help through the maze'

User feedback and consultation

2.42 Many users of adult services are satisfied with the services they receive. The Joint Reviews carried out so far show that an average of 71 per cent of service users rate the service received as excellent or good. However, this average covers a range from 84 per cent down to 59 per cent. And many users and carers report that they have not even been asked how things are going once they are receiving services.

2.43 More widely, service users and carers often play little or no part in shaping services. Attempts at consultation can often turn out to be public relations exercises, rather than genuine attempts to listen to what people want and their views of services. Genuine consultation can not only make services more responsive but also increase public confidence and trust in the services.

Consulting and involving service users

Sandwell Metropolitan Borough Council has a joint planning group which brings together the local authority, NHS, voluntary sector and users and carers. As a result of user involvement in this group, it became clear that the traditional services were failing to meet the needs and aspirations of physically disabled people of working age.

Following consultation, Sandwell therefore set up a Disability Living Centre which is managed by service users themselves. The Centre works in partnership with disabled people and carers, young and old alike, and is committed to empowering disabled people to recognise and achieve their full potential and abilities.

Individually tailored services

2.44 The commissioning approach developed following the community care reforms has improved to a large degree authorities' ability to assess an individual's needs and tailor services according to those needs. More responsive services are now delivered in many authorities, using a mixture of public, private and voluntary service providers. But there is more to be done.

2.45 Recent reports from the Audit Commission (*Take your choice* and *The Coming of Age*), the Joint Reviews annual report, and research funded by the Department of Health and carried out by PSSRU and the Nuffield Institute for Health all identify similar concerns about authorities' commissioning processes. The main points are:

- the lack of a planned, information-based approach to commissioning, looking at population needs, mapping current provision and examining the effects of current purchasing arrangements

- budgetary arrangements that make it difficult for care managers to put together a tailored care service for individuals

- the need for better relationships with both independent providers (with whom relations are sometimes adversarial) and in-house providers (where quality control is characteristically poor)

- crude systems for setting contract prices, with poor links between quality levels and the amount paid for the service.

2.46 In particular, authorities are not using the commissioning process to secure appropriate services for specific groups of people who may not be best served by mainstream services. This is especially true of people from ethnic minorities. Three recent reports, from the Racial Equality Unit (*Social care and black communities*, 1996), the Commission for Racial Equality and others (*Race, culture and community care: an agenda for action*, 1997), and the SSI (*They look after their own, don't they?*, 1998) all concluded that social services in many places were not recognising sufficiently the specific needs of ethnic minority people. Problems included language barriers, assessment procedures and services which do not recognise cultural differences, and an over-reliance on the willingness and capacity of black families and carers to look after each other.

'social services not recognising sufficiently the specific needs of ethnic minority people'

"Sometimes older people and their carers do not appear to have as much influence over their care as they should. In practice, care managers have limited choice to offer older people. Social services departments should ensure that care managers have greater influence over services by reducing restrictions on choice, introducing service level agreements with in-house providers and delegating budgets."

Audit Commission, "The Coming of Age", 1997

2.47 Obviously, councils work with finite resources, and a perfectly individualised care package will often not be possible. On the other hand, the evidence from Joint Reviews is that it is often the authorities that offer "one size fits all" services based around what suits the provider rather than the user, that are providing the *least* cost-effective services. If people are not getting the service that would most suit them, and the cost to local taxpayers is higher than it should be, then everyone is losing.

Action

2.48 Developing services that are more sensitive to individual needs, and putting the user at the heart of all social services, can only be delivered at local level. Councils must tackle these issues in partnership with other agencies, and importantly, in partnership with their local communities. Central government action in the following areas will help to ensure that this happens:

- development of a Long-term Care Charter

- work to make services easier and more convenient to use, including better information and consultation arrangements

- initiatives to improve commissioning and to make social services more responsive to individual needs.

'if people are not getting the service that would most suit them, and the cost to local taxpayers is higher than it should be, then everyone is losing'

"They look after their own, don't they?"

This SSI report was based on inspection visits to eight local authorities to look at services for ethnic minority older people. Examples of good practice were found in all visited authorities. However, the report also illustrates particular problems. For example:

- service choice was limited in many areas, and in some instances, basic services like meals-on-wheels were delivered in an inappropriate manner

- some local ethnic minority groups and agencies had developed innovative and effective ways of meeting the needs of ethnic minority elders and carers, but were not given the information, advice and support they needed to compete effectively for contracts

- where services were specifically commissioned for ethnic minority older people, they tended to be less intensive and for people with lower dependency needs. People with, say, severe cognitive impairment could be poorly served by the help they received.

Long-term Care Charter

2.49 We will introduce next year a Long-term Care Charter to set out more clearly at national level what people – both users and carers – can expect if they need support from health, housing and social services; and also what individuals' own responsibilities are in their dealings with the agencies.

2.50 The purpose of the Charter will be twofold:

- **to empower users and carers** – by promoting awareness of local services; making it clear how agencies should respond to their needs; and providing information to help users and their carers pose the right questions to the agencies they come into contact with

- to **give authorities a tool against which they can set their local standards** and which can be used by those monitoring authorities' overall performance.

2.51 Users and carers themselves are contributing to the preparation of the Charter through a series of consultation groups, so that it can concentrate on the key areas of concern for them. We are also having discussions with a variety of statutory, professional and voluntary organisations and with front-line staff. This will ensure that we have a practical document on which we intend to consult formally early next year, with a view to publishing the final Charter in the Autumn. We intend to monitor progress on the Charter through the performance frameworks for health, social services and housing.

Developing the Long-term Care Charter

The Government has been consulting with a very wide range of stakeholders to make sure that the Long-term Care Charter tackles the areas that people want it to, but so that it is also realistic and achievable. Our proposed approach to the Charter will:

- require local agencies to set standards in key areas

- tell local people the type of standard they can expect

- improve standards by empowering users and carers and through effective performance management

- improve transparency and accountability in long-term care services.

Making services easier and more convenient to use

2.52 We want to see easily-accessible services that do not make it difficult for someone who needs to get into the system. Clear and comprehensive information services are part of the answer, but it is also important that the system works together effectively for the benefit of users. We should not expect frail or vulnerable people to have to shop around for services, dealing separately with social services, housing, community health services and other agencies. When people get passed from pillar to post, it is a great cause of grievance and frustration. It is for agencies to collaborate, to ensure that an approach to one will automatically trigger contributions from partner agencies as required. This "one-stop shop" arrangement can help users to get all the services they need, whichever door they first use.

2.53 We will work to make this "one-stop shop" approach the norm in social services and other public agencies. It is at the heart of the Government's Better Government for Older People initiative (see box at the end of 2.54). We expect it to be a key feature of the Long-term Care Charter. And it is central to our plans for better joint working between the NHS and social services, with GPs, community nurses, hospitals and social services staff all working together to give people the service they need.

2.54 Through Health Improvement Programmes, which are to be introduced from April 1999 (see Chapter 6), we will expect the NHS and local authorities to develop plans for ensuring that services are coordinated and easily-accessible, linking services and using "one-stop shops" where appropriate. We will then make this a key area to be looked at by Joint Reviews, and by the local user satisfaction surveys that we will be introducing (see paragraph 2.56).

One-stop shops

Knowsley Metropolitan Borough Council opened the first of four one-stop shops in 1993. All are in convenient and accessible locations, usually in main shopping areas, The one-stop shops provide a single point of access not only to all council services but also other partner agencies, including community health services and the Benefits Agency.

The one-stop shops mean that Knowsley is able to deliver a service organised around people not buildings. For instance, a homeless man presented himself at 4.30pm on a Friday. The front-line member of staff recognised him as potentially vulnerable. With the support of housing, social services and finance staff, the man was admitted to an alcohol dependency unit that evening for rehabilitation. He left the one-stop shop with both the professional support and personal welfare rights advice he needed.

Better Government for Older People

The Better Government for Older People initiative is a central programme covering all the public services that older people regularly deal with, of which social services are an important part. The programme aims to:

- simplify access to services

- improve linkages between services provided for older people by a range of agencies

- provide clearer and more accessible information on older people's rights

- give older people a better say in the type of services they can get and make better use of the contributions they can make.

Twenty pilot projects have been set up around the country. These will be evaluated and a best practice guide published in April 2000.

'Best Value will place a requirement on local authorities to find out what local citizens' service needs are, and what they think of how the council is doing'

Information and consultation

2.55 Better information for the public will also make it easier for people to know how to go about getting social services. And consultation with both service users and the wider public will help councils to be sure that they are meeting their local population's needs.

2.56 The Best Value regime will place a requirement on local authorities to find out what local citizens' service needs are, and what they think of how the council is doing. This gives councils an opportunity to develop more regular monitoring and more effective feedback systems so that they can see how well they are doing, and whether their services are getting better from one year to the next.

2.57 As part of the new arrangements for monitoring social services performance every council will carry out local surveys of user and carer experience of and satisfaction with social services. Whilst we will not be prescriptive about the detail of these surveys, we do intend to introduce a small set of questions that will be used by all authorities, and to get them to report the responses to the Department of Health. We will then make this information available through the new Performance Assessment Framework (see Chapter 7) to allow local authorities to compare their own performance in this area with that of others and to allow the Government to monitor progress nationally. We will work closely with local authorities in drawing up detailed proposals for a common set of questions for user and carer satisfaction surveys.

Emergency and out of hours services

2.58 Most social services are ongoing in nature, but councils need to make sure that they have proper systems for responding to emergencies when they arise. They need to provide reliable and sufficient emergency and out of hours services, in particular for mentally ill people, for urgent family situations where there are risks to children, and where medical or other emergencies affecting, for instance, an elderly person may lead to a need for immediate social services help. It is important that service users are informed of out of hours and emergency services so that they know how to get help quickly in a crisis – the need for good information and easy access is all the greater in such circumstances.

2.59 The SSI is currently undertaking an inspection of the provision of emergency and out of hours services in a sample of local authorities. They will be looking, among other things, at telephone helplines and the role that they can play. The findings will help all authorities in reviewing the way they manage, resource and deliver these services.

Services centred on users: listening to people

The following case example is taken from the findings of the Joint Review of Liverpool Social Services (July 1998). It illustrates how a better outcome can be achieved through user involvement.

Mrs X, a 72 year old lady is becoming frail but is cared for by her son who lives with her, and by other local family members.

October 1995:	GP refers Mrs X to social services for home help which she declines "We're managing well and we don't need it"
December 1995:	GP refers again for home help – Mrs X accepts temporarily while her son is away
June 1997:	Mrs X has a stroke and falls – accepts home help and subsequently admitted to hospital
September 1997:	case conference: "the medical and social work consensus was for residential care – all agreed except Mrs X" (Cases file) Weekly cost £335
	Mrs X accepts package of home help – 1 hour 3 times daily
December 1997:	when visited by the review team Mrs X was delighted to still be in her home and her condition continues to improve. Weekly cost of care for the authority is less than half the cost of residential care.

Improving commissioning

'better commissioning will help to ensure that services meet people's specific individual needs, and that groups with particular needs, such as people from ethnic minorities, are better served'

2.60 Better commissioning will help to ensure that services meet people's specific individual needs, and that groups with particular needs, such as people from ethnic minorities, are better served. We shall ensure that authorities improve the standard of their commissioning by:

- publishing guidance around the turn of the year setting out the kind of information councils need to improve the impact of their commissioning. This will be based on a study of information needs carried out by the Department of Health, and will complement Audit Commission work.

- issuing a self audit tool to help councils review their care management arrangements, including how purchasing activities of care managers can better inform commissioning

- using Best Value service reviews, Joint Reviews and SSI Inspections to ensure that best practice is being implemented

- raising awareness about good practice through a series of workshops (a process we have already begun).

Four key elements of good commissioning

Needs analysis: commissioning should be based on an assessment of need within the general population that is thorough and based on local evidence. Where appropriate such assessments of need should cover not only social care, but also health, housing and other aspects. Information about gaps in services, services which users would prefer, service shortfalls, and provider performance (through contract monitoring) should be systematically collected during referral and assessment processes, and fed into planning processes.

Strategic planning: planning and planned changes should be in pursuit of agreed strategic objectives, and the planning process should be transparent to users and providers. Information about need, supply and service use should collected by commissioners, and fed into the planning process. It should be shared with providers and user and carer groups. The views and wishes of users and carers should be systematically sought, and fed into planning processes. Providers from all sectors should be encouraged, and provided with relevant information. Commissioners should ensure that commissioning funds are flexible and can be switched as required from services that are no longer needed to new ones that are.

Contract setting and market management: a variety of contract types should be used to deliver positive outcomes for users and reasonable security for good providers. Good commissioners should have mechanisms for stimulating new services where needs have been identified, and services are not available. Such mechanisms could involve some form of 'pump priming' such as the use of a block contract to reward a provider for providing new service with a guaranteed level of income. Contract prices should not be set mechanistically but with regard to providers' costs and planned outcomes for users.

Contract monitoring: general contracts and specific contracts should be monitored to ensure that providers are providing acceptable standards of care, and that individuals are receiving appropriate help at agreed prices. Commissioners should ensure that providers have their own quality assurance and control systems in place. Good commissioners take swift remedial action when contract monitoring or other information points to problems with individual providers or with a sector of the market. Contracts should be constructed and monitored in such a way as to enable commissioners to identify fraud and safeguard themselves against it.

2.61 An essential part of commissioning processes in future will be to ensure that the assessment of local needs takes account of Health Improvement Programmes (see Chapter 6). Strategic planning for local social services must fit closely together with these wider programmes for improving health.

How will people see the benefits of our changes?

'services that are suited to the needs of people, not the convenience of providers'

2.62 The benefits of a more user-centred approach to social services should be seen in:

- services that are suited to the needs of people, not the convenience of providers

- clearer information for the public on services and standards, building on the Long-term Care Charter

- less confusion and bureaucracy for users and carers to contend with, through better access arrangements and "one-stop shops"

- more choice, and services better suited to individual needs, based on improved user feedback and improved commissioning processes

- better targeted services for people from ethnic minorities

- an increase in service users' satisfaction levels, as measured in local surveys.

> *All authorities will carry out local user satisfaction surveys, starting from April 2000.*

Conclusion

2.63 All these measures, taken together with the proposals on regulation, on closer partnership working and on improved performance management outlined elsewhere in this White Paper, will set out a significant agenda for modernisation and improvement in adult social services over the coming years. The new pattern of social services for adults will be one where people will:

- understand how to get access to services, what is available for their level of needs, and what their own contribution might be

- be involved, with their carers, in working out support arrangements

- be confident that the support that is agreed will help them to lead their own lives as far as possible, to continue to live in their own home, and to do as much for themselves as possible

- be confident that if they lived in another area, the support they would get, and any contribution they make, would be similar.

'these measures set out a significant agenda for modernisation and improvement in adult social services'

3

Key themes

- *new, stronger systems for protecting children*
- *"Quality Protects" – improving quality across all children's services*
- *better health and education for children in care homes, and more help for young people leaving care*

Services for children

protection, quality of care, improving life chances

Introduction

3.1 All local authority services have an impact on children's lives – whether to ensure a high standard of education, or a safe and healthy environment for them to live in, or to provide safe places to play. The whole local authority has a contribution to make to children's services. But those children and families who need the help of social services are likely to be amongst the most vulnerable and excluded in our society – children in need, disabled children, children who need protection, children in trouble with the law, children who need to be cared for away from home.

'standards of delivery and achievement are unreliable, and though many children benefit from social services, too many are let down'

3.2 Local authorities have very particular responsibilities towards these children and their families. Nowhere is the challenge of social services work better illustrated. The decisions are hard, and the consequences of misjudgment serious – whether this means removing a child from their family without good cause or leaving a child too long in a dangerous setting. Many authorities have the right intentions in their approach to this difficult field; and many people working in it bring skill and dedication to what they do. But there is ample evidence, from recent SSI and Joint Review reports, from the Children's Safeguards Review, and from the recent report on Looked After Children by the Health Select Committee, that standards of delivery and achievement are unreliable, and that though many children benefit from social services, too many are let down.

3.3 Working in partnership with local authorities and the voluntary sector, the Government is determined to raise standards for children who need the active support of social services. The Government is providing the necessary leadership, guidance and funding for local authorities to implement our demanding agenda for action. For their part, local authorities will be required to draw up and follow individual action plans to achieve a range of targets. The Government will closely monitor developments and, as necessary, pursue authorities where standards are not acceptable.

The wider agenda

3.4 Social services for children cannot be seen in isolation from the wider range of children's services delivered by local authorities and other agencies. The Government is committed to taking action through a broad range of initiatives to strengthen family life, to reduce social exclusion and anti-social behaviour among children, and to give every child the opportunity of a healthy, happy, successful life. Examples of Government action on the wider front include the "Sure Start" programme, the Crime Reduction Programme, Early Years Development and Childcare Partnerships and the Green Paper *Supporting Families*.

3.5 Children's social services must be seen within this wider context. However, this must not mean that social services lose their focus on the most vulnerable children. Too many reports and inquiries have highlighted cases where social services have failed vulnerable children. Children in the care of local authorities have been abused and neglected by the care system that was supposed to look after them. Children placed on a child protection register have had no monitoring or checks – despite being specifically identified as being at risk. And the majority of looked after children leave care with no educational qualification at all, many of them at great risk of falling into unemployment, homelessness, crime and prostitution.

3.6 The Government is determined to tackle these serious shortcomings, and has already begun the process of addressing the priority areas for improvement.

"... concerns have been highlighted graphically in recent inspection work on planning and decision making both for children in need and children looked after. We found it was unusual for families to be assessed systematically taking account of their strengths and weaknesses. Departments more often simply responded to the problem that was presented. As a result some families who needed support were inappropriately caught up in the child protection system, whilst in other situations obvious risks to children were overlooked. Poor planning meant that many children looked after experienced unacceptably long delays before placement was made. Too many children who were the responsibility of the local authority did not have a social worker assigned to them or a proper care plan. Record keeping ranged from very good to abysmal. It was often not possible to see why social services had intervened, what they hoped to achieve and how they would know whether the situation had improved or deteriorated. This is unacceptable"

Social Services Facing the Future, the 1997/98 annual report of the Chief Inspector, Social Services Inspectorate.

'the Government is determined to tackle these serious shortcomings, and has already begun the process of addressing the priority areas for improvement'

Children and families: the wider agenda

"Sure Start" is a new initiative to help give children the best possible start in life, particularly those in disadvantaged areas. In England, over £450m over the next three years will be targeted on the areas of greatest need, building on what is already provided in the health, education, social services and voluntary sector.

The Government's **Crime Reduction Programme,** like "Sure Start", will include work through local partnerships to tackle social exclusion and anti-social behaviour among children and young people. £250m of funding will be available over the next three years for the programme as a whole.

Early Years Development and Childcare Plans provide a focus for planning integrated education and care services for children and their families.

The Green Paper *Supporting Families*, published on 4 November 1998, set out the wider agenda for all government action to strengthen family life and improve opportunities for children.

The priorities

3.7 As with adult services, new objectives have been defined at a national level for children's social services. They are set out in Chapter 7. The Government's plans for radical improvement target three priority aims:

- to ensure that children are **protected** from sexual, physical and emotional abuse, and from neglect

- to **raise the quality of care** of children in care so that it is as close as possible to the care provided by loving and responsible parents

- to **improve the life chances** of children in care, and of others ("children in need") who need social services' support, in particular through improving their health and education and support after they leave care.

Protection

3.8 Nobody knows with any certainty how much serious harm and abuse is suffered by children within their own families, or in residential homes, foster care, boarding schools and other settings where children live away from home. We cannot know whether the amount of abuse suffered by children has increased or fallen over the years. For many years, abuse – particularly sexual abuse – was a taboo subject and allegations made by children and young people were not listened to. Public and professional awareness is now much greater. But children often still lack the power and opportunity to voice what is happening to them, and the adults responsible have every motive to conceal it.

3.9 But we do know that:

- the risks to children living away from home in residential homes, foster care and residential schools in the 1970s and 1980s were seriously under-estimated. The numbers of convictions of care workers, of serious investigations into allegations of crimes from this period and the testimony of adult survivors all paint a shocking picture

- too many children die or suffer serious injury at the hands of adult abusers. In 1997/98 the Department of Health received reports of 91 such cases

- most families who become caught up in the child protection system are at high risk of social exclusion. The SSI report, *Child Protection: Messages From Research*, shows that many have multiple problems – poverty, family breakdown, mental health problems, domestic violence, alcohol and drug misuse – which need careful assessment and targeted intervention by local authorities to ensure that children are not put at risk.

Protection of looked after children

3.10 Failures to protect children in residential settings and in foster care are only too well known. The case of Frank Beck in Leicestershire, and the "Pindown" practices in Staffordshire, brought the issue to the public eye in the 1980s. Other scandals that have come to light in recent years also relate to abuse carried out in the 1970s and 1980s, but we cannot be complacent that such problems have been eradicated. Last year saw the convictions of Keith Laverack, who abused children in several homes in recent years, and of Roger Saint, a foster carer convicted of sexual abuse. The Tribunal of Inquiry into cases of child abuse in North Wales is expected to report shortly.

'failures to protect children in residential settings and in foster care are only too well known'

3.11 These failures have several causes:

- there have been gaps in the **regulatory safeguards** around residential homes and schools, and in the arrangements for monitoring foster care. Some of these were addressed in the Children Act 1989 and associated regulations and guidance, but significant weaknesses remain. Small private children's homes are excluded from regulation though their number has increased. Independent boarding schools are inspected for social welfare, but maintained residential schools are not. There are no regulatory safeguards applying to independent fostering agencies.

- safeguards against the **appointment or retention of unsuitable people** in work with children have improved since the report *Choosing with Care* by Norman Warner. But the recent SSI report, *Someone Else's Children*, found that local authority practice is by no means uniformly rigorous and reliable and has not been consistently applied to foster care. The process for obtaining checks is too long and complex – employers have to make several applications to check criminal records and other sources including the Department of Health's *Consultancy Index* (see box in paragraph 3.18) to ensure that they have all the information available. There has been no exchange of information on health care workers moving into the social services who should be excluded from such work.

- **too many children are placed a long way away** from their homes and are not properly monitored by their care authorities. The 1997 SSI survey on the safety of children in the public care found that one-fifth of children looked after were living outside the area of their care authority. Of these, 900 were reported to be placed more than 150 miles away. The survey suggested a substantial majority of councils had given less than satisfactory thought to ensuring required procedures for placement and review in "out of authority" cases were carried out properly.

'safeguards against the appointment or retention of unsuitable people in work with children'

Child protection in family settings

3.12 In recent years there have been improvements in procedures for child protection and in cooperation between agencies. Area Child Protection Committees have done much to foster strong partnerships in many areas. However, *Messages From Inspection,* an overview of SSI's major child protection inspection programme between 1992 and 1996, found that while the great majority of local authorities provide some examples of good practice, only a small minority of local authorities provide good quality services across the whole range of children's work. Overall it remains the case that most children and their families are not as well served as they should be.

3.13 Some of the reasons for this failure are:

- poor assessment and case planning with a tendency identified in *Someone Else's Children* to continue attempts at rehabilitation for some children in dangerous family settings for longer than is safe to do so

- poor case recording practices

- child protection plans which are often lacking in focus and not followed up systematically. This can result in children moving on and off the child protection register without a lasting improvement in their circumstances

- failure to ensure that all children on the child protection register have an allocated social worker

- weaknesses in the supervision of staff and the monitoring of the quality of practice

- shortcomings in the training and experience of staff.

'while the great majority of local authorities provide some examples of good practice, only a small minority of local authorities provide good quality services across the whole range of children's work'

3.14 Serious professional failings such as these have resulted in tragedies. The terrible cases set out in the box below were, when investigated, found to illustrate wider failings in the local authority's and other agencies' child protection system.

Rikki Neave was killed in 1995 at the age of 6, after a long history of abuse and neglect by his family. Social services had a long history of involvement, but failed to take decisive action to protect Rikki and his siblings. At one point, Rikki's name was on the child protection register but was removed. When he died, his name was not on the register.

Leanne White, who died in 1992 at the age of three, provides an example where social services staff failed to listen to concerns of relatives. Social services were too trusting and accepted plausible accounts provided by adults at face value. Despite being told by seven different people about her plight, social services failed to take adequate action. Leanne was found to have 107 separate injuries at the time of her death.

Karl Speke came from a large and deprived family with inadequate and neglectful parents. The family moved around the country at least 11 times to avoid the attentions of the agencies involved with them. The father was aggressive and violent and succeeded in intimidating staff from all agencies. Karl was killed in 1996 at the age of two. He had not been seen by social services or by health staff for 17 months before his death. Communication between health and social services was poor.

Action

3.15 Government action to improve the protection of children includes:

- root and branch reform of the regulation system, introducing checks on the full range of children's care services, and strengthening safeguards

- an extensive range of reforms, set out in the Government's response to the Children's Safeguards Review, to improve the protection of all children living away from home

- stronger systems for preventing unsuitable people from working with children

- a thorough revision of the Government guidance on child protection.

Regulation reform

3.16 The detail of these changes are set out in Chapter 4. For children's services the key points are:

- a new independent regulatory system, ending the situation where the local authority is both the purchaser and the inspector

- full powers of inspection and enforcement for all children's homes, including homes run by local authorities

- new protections in services not currently covered – small children's homes, state sector boarding schools, residential family centres and independent fostering agencies

- new national standards for regulation, replacing the inconsistencies of the current system.

'introducing checks on the full range of children's care services, and strengthening safeguards'

'new national standards for regulation, replacing the inconsistencies of the current system'

Response to the Children's Safeguards Review

3.17 The Government's response to the Children's Safeguards Review (see opposite) covered the full range of action to be taken to improve the lives of children living away from home. Many of these are set out elsewhere in this chapter (strengthened regulation, better arrangements for stopping dangerous people from working with children, revised child protection guidance, enhanced inter-agency working, and the "Quality Protects" programme). In addition to all of these, the Government's response also made the following commitments for improving protection:

- ensure proper complaints procedures exist in all residential care settings

- provide information to protect and educate young people on unsafe practices and situations, and ensure they know how to contact outside help to raise concerns

- ensure all children statutorily entitled to independent visitors are provided with one

- promote the involvement of children in decisions on their care, local planning and national policy making

- funding for a group to provide a national voice for children in care and those formerly in care, and to promote their interests;

- publish National Standards for Foster Care in 1999

- issue statutory guidance on action to be taken when a looked after child goes missing

- remind all governing bodies of organisations responsible for the care of children that they should have procedures to enable staff to raise significant concerns outside normal line management structures

- undertake an information campaign for parents on the dangers that can be faced by children living away from home.

'provide information to protect and educate young people on unsafe practices and situations, and ensure they know how to contact outside help to raise concerns'

'procedures to enable staff to raise significant concerns outside normal line management structures'

The Children's Safeguards Review

In November 1997, the Government published the report of the Review of the Safeguards for Children Living Away from Home. This review followed reports of widespread abuse of children in care.

Although the main focus of the report was children looked after by local authorities (there are about 55,000 of them at any time), it also covers safeguards for other children living away from home, for example, in boarding schools and penal settings. In all, about 200,000 of the 12 million children under the age of 18 in England and Wales are living away from their parents' home for at least 28 days.

The report makes 20 principal recommendations, and over 130 other recommendations, the aims of which include:

- improve protection for children in foster and residential care, in schools and in the penal system

- provide more effective safeguards and checks to deter abusers from working with children

- improve outcomes and life chances of all children, particularly those looked after by local authorities

- reduce the numbers of young people leaving care early and increase the support, advice and assistance available to them

- provide more effective avenues of complaint and increase access to independent advocates

- provide more vigilant management

- provide effective disciplinary and criminal procedures

- provide effective systems of communication between agencies about known abusers.

The Government's response, setting out action on all these fronts, was published on 5 November 1998.

Stopping dangerous people from working with children

'the Government will take further steps to prevent unsuitable people from working with children'

3.18 The Government will take further steps to prevent unsuitable people from working with children. We will:

- establish a new Criminal Records Agency to improve and widen access to police checks on people intending to work with children and other vulnerable groups. For those who have regular access to children, this will disclose details of all convictions of all offences (whether or not they are "spent") and details of any cautions recorded on the national records, as well as any relevant non-conviction information. This will be a first step towards a "one-stop shop" which will give employers access to police records and the separate lists kept by the Department for Education and Employment (List 99) and the Department of Health (the Consultancy Index)

- in the interim, introduce legislation when Parliamentary time allows, to place the Consultancy Index on a statutory basis; to clarify the procedure for representations against inclusion on the Index; to make inclusion on the Index a bar to employment in the relevant fields; and to extend the Index to cover child care staff working in certain areas of the NHS

- enforce full compliance by social services authorities with the recommendations of *Choosing with Care* and adopt these principles in other settings where children live away from home

- create a new statutory General Teaching Council which will have registration and disciplinary powers over teachers; and through future legislation create a General Social Care Council (see Chapter 5) which will set the conduct and practice standards for the whole social care workforce and in due course register those working with children.

3.19 The Government has established an Inter-Departmental Working Group, led by the Home Office, to look at how to prevent those considered unsuitable to work with children from gaining work with them. The work will cover the public, private and voluntary sectors and will draw on measures already in existence.

The Consultancy Index

The Department of Health Consultancy Service Index enables local authorities and private and voluntary child care organisations in England and Wales to check on the suitability of those they propose to employ. It is a list of people about whom concerns exist around their suitability for work in the child care field. It is used by child care employers when considering the employment of people to posts involving substantial, unsupervised access to children. Information is supplied by employers when staff are dismissed or resign in certain circumstances. The Index also maintains a list of child care workers whose names have been notified to the Department by the Police following certain convictions and cautions.

New child protection guidance

3.20 The Government has made clear that it intends to strengthen its guidance on child protection procedures and the arrangements for cooperation and partnership between agencies. While the existing guidance, *Working Together Under The Children Act 1989*, has made a start, we believe that more needs to be done to break down barriers, and to promote a wider, more holistic view of the needs of vulnerable children to ensure that children are not unnecessarily drawn into child protection and court procedures. We must also strengthen the safeguards that the child protection system offers to all children, whether living with their families or away from home.

3.21 Earlier this year the Department of Health issued a consultation paper inviting views on the scope and contents of the new guidance. This has generated a lively debate about the way forward with over 650 responses. The Government intends to issue new guidance by the Spring of 1999. This will be accompanied by a new framework for undertaking needs-led assessment of children and their families.

3.22 As part of the Quality Protects programme (see paragraph 3.25), local authorities must take action to bring their child protection services up to standard. They will be required to show that they:

- carry out thorough and prompt assessments of children's needs

- have good case records

- draw up and implement child protection plans which are then reviewed regularly

- ensure that all children on the child protection register have an allocated social worker

- know what outcomes they want for children in need of protection and assess whether these are being achieved

- have a human resources strategy which identifies the skills and knowledge needed by child protection staff.

'know what outcomes they want for children in need of protection and assess whether these are being achieved'

'children's services will continue to receive the closest scrutiny'

3.23 We intend to make sure that children's services continue to receive the closest scrutiny to ensure that children are safeguarded against harm. The Government will therefore put in place new arrangements whereby from time to time it will commission from all its Chief Inspectors of services substantially involved with children (the SSI, Ofsted, and the Inspectorates for Prisons, Probation and the Police) a single joint report on children's safeguards. This will enable the Government to satisfy itself that the safeguards for children across the range of services are being properly implemented, and that the safety of children continues to be given the priority it deserves. These reports will be produced every three years, or more often if required, and will be published. Aside from these reports, the inspectorates will work together as a matter of course on issues related to children's safeguards.

How will people see the benefits of our changes?

With a determined effort to improve both the legal framework for protection and the way in which authorities undertake their responsibilities for children, we should see:

- much tighter checks against abuse of children in care. We may never be able to eradicate abuse completely, but we can put an end to those cases where weaknesses in the system allow the abuse to go undetected, or fail to stamp it out effectively when discovered

- dangerous people effectively kept out of jobs with contact with children

- better handling of cases where a child may be at risk at home – schools, hospitals, and others who work with families will have clearer guidance on how to work with social services in these cases. And better procedures will mean that children no longer drift on and off the child protection register with no real improvement in their situation.

By 2002, the proportion of children who are re-registered on the child protection register will be reduced by 10% compared to the year ending March 1997.

Quality of care

3.24 Local authorities in England now look after some 55,000 children at any one time, and in any single year they accept responsibility for about 88,000 children, many of them for relatively short periods. When they accept the responsibility for looking after a child, whether by a court order or through an agreement with the child's parents, a local authority has an obligation to provide personal care and to support the child's development, help to access suitable health and education services, and protect the child's safety in the same way as any other responsible parent. They should aim, so far as is possible, to give the child the same chance of a fulfilling life as other children have. Evidence from inspections and other sources describe weaknesses in a number of aspects of local authority services for children:

- children are often not properly assessed when they first present for help, and many drift through a variety of short-term placements. Published Department of Health Statistics show that 10,300 children (that is 20%) looked after by authorities on 31 March 1997 had experienced three or more placements in the course of the previous year. An unpublished estimate from the same source suggests that about 2,000 of these had 6 or more placements. A settled life for a child in such circumstances is impossible

- many authorities do not have clear eligibility criteria for services. Families with disabled children are faced with a series of obstacles to overcome before receiving help. The help provided is often determined more by what service was readily available than a proper assessment of the family's needs

- there are weaknesses in the scale and type of fostering and residential care placement options, particularly for children with highly specialised needs

- there is evidence that adoption is regarded by some authorities as an option of last resort

- the quality of management, assessment and decision-taking in the public care system is patchy and unreliable. It can be as damaging to take a child into care unnecessarily as it can be to fail to take action

"The quality of assessment was extremely variable not only between Social Services Departments (SSDs) but also within SSDs There was often an abundance of information gathering which was unstructured and it was difficult to discern how decisions were derived from it."

"Every SSD had a problem in ensuring compliance with its policies and procedures and in addressing variability in practice."

"Only 9 out of 27 SSDs had care plans on all files."

"Many of the plans lacked detail or were out of date."

Someone Else's Children, SSI 1998

'local authorities should aim, so far as is possible, to give the child in public care the same chance of a fulfilling life as other children have'

- many authorities have weaknesses in strategic planning and financial management

- while some authorities are making useful headway, many do not adequately identify trends in need and demand. Nor do they adequately assess and prioritise need and target services on the most serious problems. These are difficult issues requiring expertise which many authorities do not currently have

- there is a lack of good information on costs and outcomes. Information on the services provided is not matched up with information on expenditure. Only a very few authorities have developed their own systems to analyse costs and none have related expenditure to outcomes. This makes it difficult, nationally and locally, to judge whether best value is being obtained from the £2.25 billion a year spent by social services on services for children.

Action

'a major initiative, called Quality Protects'

3.25 To tackle these problems, and to address all aspects of children's social services, the Government has already launched a major initiative, called Quality Protects. This is a three-year programme to remedy the defects in the standards of care offered to looked after children and other children needing social services' support. It will tackle problems of attitudes, standards, management, service delivery and training.

3.26 To support the Quality Protects programme the Government will make available £375 million of extra resources from the Social Services Modernisation Fund over the next three years. The amount of this Children's Services Grant in 1999/2000 will be £75m. It will rise to £120m in the following year and to £180m in 2001/2002.

3.27 Payments under the Children's Services Grant will be subject to the preparation and achievement of satisfactory action plans by each local authority. By 31 January 1999 each authority will be required to assess its performance in a number of key areas and propose action to remedy deficiencies. The grant will also fund eight regional development workers who will help authorities examine their need for reform, disseminate materials and methods, and exchange expertise and experience.

3.28 It is clear that while some issues will require immediate action on the part of authorities, others will require longer term initiatives. Key areas of work linked to improving the management of children's services in general, and strategic and financial management in particular, include:

- better systems for assessing children's needs in communities

- strengthening the planning of children's services by making it a council-wide function (see Chapter 6 for further detail)

- ensuring, through the national objectives for children's social services, and the National Priorities Guidance, that all services are working to common objectives and priorities

- introduction of a national collection of expenditure returns across all children and families served, in a way that generates financial management information authorities need for their own purposes

- dissemination of research relevant to the management of children's services, and the improvement of senior and middle management capability

- introduction of quality assurance monitoring and internal auditing practices

- identifying centres of good practice to act as beacons for spreading excellence in children's services.

'it is clear that while some issues will require immediate action on the part of authorities, others will require longer term initiatives'

'identifying centres of good practice to act as beacons for spreading excellence in children's services'

Action to improve adoption services

Adoption should be seen as a positive option. There is good evidence from research that in the right circumstances adoption has good outcomes, and that the younger the child at the time of adoption the better the outcome. The Government has already issued fresh guidance designed to:

- bring back the adoption service into the mainstream of child care practice

- break down prejudices against the principle of adoption

- challenge rigid attitudes in the transracial placement of children for adoption if they are carried to the point of withholding the potential benefit of an adoption from a child simply because it cannot be matched with parents of the same ethnic group.

The Government will keep the working of the adoption service under careful review, and will consider whether fresh legislation would help to overcome some of the delays without denying the rights of birth families to take part in the process.

3.29 Service issues to be addressed as part of the initiative will include:

- improvements in assessment and decision making through further development and implementation of the assessment and planning tool *Looking After Children*, and publication of a new assessment model for children and families in need in the community

- use of the Children's Services Grant to review the supply of residential and fostering placements and take action, including greater support for recruitment and retention of foster carers and where necessary residential provision, and working in consortia to provide specialist placements

- identifying the needs and expectations of children and carers by involving children in decisions on their care, involving young people in developing policy, local strategies and staff training, and encouraging the provision by local authorities of children's rights services and independent visitors.

How will people see the benefits of our changes?

The Government's reforms and the Quality Protects initiative will lead to a transformation of children's social services. In relation to the quality of care, the key outcomes will be:

- clearer objectives for all actions taken by social services for children – if a child has to leave his/her family, social services will ensure that this is the best option, and will act as any decent parent would in making sure that the child's best interests are being met

- more stable care relationships for children looked after, with minimal disruption from being moved between placements

By 2001 all authorities will match the performance of the top quarter, so that the percentage of children looked after who have 3 or more placements in one year will be no more than 16%.

- a wider range of foster care placements and residential accommodation in order to meet children's specific needs; and consideration of adoption in any case where a return to the child's own family will not be possible

- greatly improved management arrangements for children's social services, with better quality planning, assessment and decision-making in all areas.

Improved life chances

3.30 Although much has happened to disadvantage many children prior to their needing to be looked after, the fact remains that the outcomes for children in the care of local authorities are disappointing. Only with good assessment, well thought out and durable placements, proper planning for independence and partnership with other agencies can these children be offered the opportunities they are entitled to. All too often these have not been made available.

3.31 Information from the Looking After Children Programme suggests that while many children and young people have significantly greater health needs than their peers in the community they have greater difficulties in getting access to services. This is related both to the number of placements at some distance from the responsible authority, and also to the frequency of moves which interferes with prompt NHS treatment. Social services, education and the NHS do not work well enough together, the quality of services for care leavers is patchy, and the quality of assessment and planning does not always reach the levels we expect. The outcome of all this is that the life chances of children in care are unacceptably low, with poor opportunities while in care and low chances of successful settled lives once they leave care:

- an estimated 30% of children looked after have statements of special educational need, compared with 2-3% of children generally

- in some authorities as few as 25% of young people leave care with any educational qualification.

- one in four children looked after aged 14-16 do not attend school regularly and many have been excluded and have no regular educational placement

- 67% of children looked after have an identifiable mental health problem

'the life chances of children in care are unacceptably low, with poor opportunities while in care and low chances of successful settled lives once they leave care'

'between 14% and 25% of young women leaving care are pregnant or have a child'

- between 14% and 25% of young women leaving care are either pregnant or have a child, while in the general population only 3% of 20 year old women have a child

- up to a third of people sleeping rough have been looked after by local authorities at some point in their childhood

- 39% of male prisoners under 21, and 22% of all male prisoners, have been looked after by local authorities at some point in their childhood.

3.32 Good parents do not abandon their children unaided to face the challenges and chances of life alone at the age of sixteen or even eighteen. They continue to support them with advice, guidance and where necessary money. Many local authorities do make significant efforts to provide continuing support to young people who have spent considerable periods in public care. The SSI reported last year that it had found many examples of creative and innovative practice, especially in partnership with the voluntary sector. However, it also found that provision was patchy and that some areas offered poor services for care leavers.

Action

3.33 Government action to improve the life chances of children looked after includes:

- action to improve education for looked after children

- action to improve health services for looked after children

- legislation to extend the duty of a local authority for children in care from 16 to 18 years old, and new statutory obligations on local authorities to provide for the needs of children leaving care.

Education

3.34 Good educational opportunities are essential for improved life chances. The Government has set new targets to be met by all local authorities and is providing for the targets to be incorporated in Education Development Plans. It intends to consult next year on new guidelines – eventually to be given statutory force – on the education of looked after children, applying to education and social services alike. A national forum, with representatives of leading statutory and voluntary agencies, has been looking at a range of possible initiatives to improve the education and attainment of looked after children.

3.35 Local education authorities are required to publish behaviour support plans by 31 December 1998 making reference specifically to looked-after young people and other groups who are recognised to be at risk of failing to fulfil their potential. The Government is shortly issuing for consultation new advice to help reduce exclusions and truancy. It is taking a series of initiatives to improve provision for children with emotional and behavioural difficulties, including looked after children. A particular aim is to identify emergent difficulties and intervene early to prevent them taking root.

3.36 The educational attainment of looked after children is a joint responsibility of education and social services, and the care system itself should ensure that educational opportunities are taken up. If a local authority is fulfilling parental responsibilities for its looked after children, that should extend to ensuring attendance at school, checking on the child's educational progress, attending open days at schools and so on. This is one of the areas covered by the Quality Protects initiative.

'good educational opportunities are essential for improved life chances'

Health

3.37 In the White Paper *The new NHS* the Government set out proposals for a new statutory duty of partnership to ensure that health authorities work closely with local authorities and other agencies to improve the health of the local population. Health Improvement Programmes should identify groups such as children looked after who need particular attention.

'entry to care is a key opportunity to identify the health needs of the child or young person'

3.38 Entry to care is a key opportunity to identify the health needs of the child or young person and to plan, with them, the necessary action to be taken. Guidance will be issued during 1999 to ensure that each child or young person entering care is offered a comprehensive health assessment. Particular areas for targeted health support will include improved child and adolescent mental health services; and work with young girls in care to reduce the rate of teenage pregnancies.

Care leavers

3.39 As a matter of priority public care services must be improved in order to help looked after young people move into fulfilling independent lives in as stable a fashion as possible. We have made this a specific objective in the new objectives for children's services. We will also:

- legislate when Parliamentary time allows to create new and stronger duties on councils to support care leavers up to at least 18; and we will discourage discharge below that age in cases where it is premature. The local authority's responsibilities should correspond more closely with those of parents, including keeping in touch with more young people after they have left care

- develop new arrangements for each 16 to 18 year old leaving care to have a clear plan setting out a "pathway to independence". The aim will be to develop the care leaver's life skills and help the move from care to fully independent life. Details of the new arrangements will be announced by April 1999

- improve assistance to care leavers with obtaining suitable and affordable accommodation, including issuing guidance to housing and social services on the accommodation needs of care leavers and the support they require to maintain a stable tenancy

- recognise the specific needs of those in and leaving care in the further and higher education arrangements, and in the Government's instructions to The Careers Service

- require local authorities to provide suitable accommodation for care leavers in higher education during vacations

- exempt unemployed care leavers over 18 from the six month qualifying period for acceptance onto the New Deal.

'support care leavers up to at least 18'

Improving life chances for children in care

Leicester City Council has launched the Corporate Parent Initiative, which aims to ensure that children in the council's care enjoy the same opportunities as other children.

The council has set up a group of officers who act as "champions" in their departments for looked after children. The group develops ideas and introduces improvements. Achievements to date include:

- improving educational performance
- providing low-cost housing for care leavers
- providing free passes to the council's sports and leisure facilities
- getting jobs with the council for some young people leaving care

London Borough of Newham has appointed a team of teachers to work with young people accommodated and looked after. The initiative provides homework clubs, individual support, liaison with schools, home tuition, and support to return young people to mainstream and further education.

The Royal Borough of **Kingston upon Thames** provides a range of different types of accommodation to match the individual needs of care leavers. Young people who find it difficult to live independently in flats can be moved back to shared or supported accommodation. This is achieved through strategic planning and collaborative working between social services, housing and the voluntary sector.

3.40 The Social Exclusion Unit has also been set the priority task of considering how to reduce the number of 16-18 year olds who are not in education, training and employment. This work, in addition to the Unit's reports so far on rough sleepers and neighbourhood renewal (See Chapter 6), should have a positive impact on the lifestyles of care leavers.

How will people see the benefits of our changes?

Action to improve the life chances of children looked after will result in:

- better education services for children in care, and improved educational achievement by the time a child leaves care

> *The proportion of children leaving care at sixteen or later with a GCSE or GNVQ qualification will increase to at least 50% by 2001, and to at least 75% by 2003.*

- better health services for looked after children, including comprehensive health assessment for every child on entry into care

- better support for young people making the difficult transition from the care system to independent adult life. Local authorities will help care leavers to sort out where to live, and how to move into employment or further education and training.

> *The level of employment, training or education among young people aged nineteen in 2001/02 who were looked after by local authorities in their seventeenth year on 1 April 1999 will be at least 60% of the level among all young people of the same age in their area.*

Conclusion

3.41 Proposals elsewhere in this White Paper will also have an impact on the quality of social services for children, notably:

- the changes to regulation in children's services, and the establishment of regional children's rights officers, in Chapter 4

- the child care training strategy and other workforce improvements in Chapter 5

- the proposals on children's services planning and on youth justice, in Chapter 6.

3.42 Taken together, these developments and the Government's core proposals in this Chapter will provide a new start for children's social services. We intend to ensure that in future, every child who comes into contact with social services will gain real benefit from that contact; that children and families in need can count on social services to give them the support they need; that children in care are protected from harm; and that after many years of widespread mistrust, the general public can once again have faith in our public care system. We will work with local authorities and others to make sure these aims are achieved.

'in future every child who comes into contact with social services will gain real benefit from that contact'

4

Key themes

- *new, independent system for protecting vulnerable people: Commissions for Care Standards*
- *more services covered by inspection*
- *stronger national standards*

Improving protection

new inspection systems, stronger safeguards

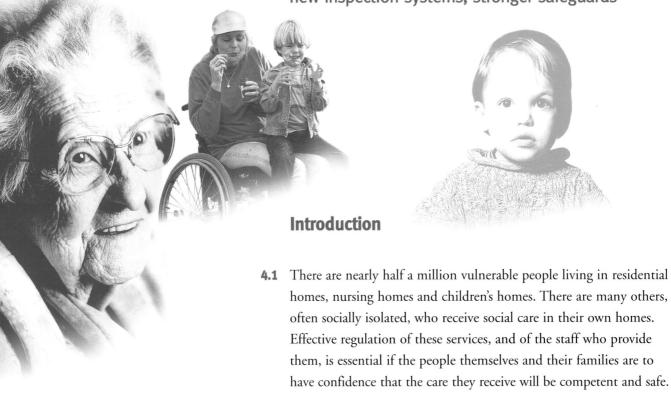

Introduction

4.1 There are nearly half a million vulnerable people living in residential homes, nursing homes and children's homes. There are many others, often socially isolated, who receive social care in their own homes. Effective regulation of these services, and of the staff who provide them, is essential if the people themselves and their families are to have confidence that the care they receive will be competent and safe.

'the present regulatory arrangements are incomplete and patchy'

4.2 The present regulatory arrangements are incomplete and patchy, and the Government will replace them with a system that is modern, independent and dependable. Taken together with the establishment of the General Social Care Council (described in Chapter 5), these reforms will put in place new systems for ensuring that when people receive care, it is safe and of high quality, that they have adequate living standards if they are in care homes, and that the staff on whom they rely have the training, skills and standards that are necessary for the work they do.

4.3 No regulatory system can absolutely guarantee consistently good standards everywhere, but we must make sure that the system we put in place does everything that is possible to prevent and root out the abuse and neglect of vulnerable people.

4.4   The Government's plans are designed with the principles of good regulation in mind. These principles, set out by the Better Regulation Task Force, are:

- transparency

- accountability

- targeting

- consistency

- proportionality.

4.5   The Better Regulation Task Force's own review of long-term care regulation, published earlier this year, concluded that the existing regulation arrangements fail on all these principles.

Problems with the current system

4.6   The existing arrangements for regulating care services have developed in a piecemeal fashion. Responsibilities for regulating the various services for adults and children are divided between local authorities, health authorities and the Department of Health centrally (see chart overleaf). Other services – notably councils' own care homes, small children's homes and domiciliary care (care given to people in their own homes) – are not subject to any regulation.

4.7   This situation leads to a number of problems:

- **lack of independence** – local and health authorities have to combine responsibilities for purchasing, providing and regulating care services. As well as the conflict of interest that this causes, this means that people in local authority care homes do not benefit from independent regulation.

- **lack of coherence** – responsibilities are split between different authorities and different professional disciplines (social services professionals on the one hand, and mostly professional nurses on the other). This means that there is not effective scrutiny of nursing care in residential homes and social care in nursing homes, for example.

'the Government's plans are designed with the principles of good regulation in mind'

- **lack of consistency** – there are 150 local authorities and 100 health authorities in England. Standards vary from one area to another, creating uncertainty for both providers and service users. For instance, different approaches are taken to room sizes, numbers and training of staff, and the maximum number of places allowed in a home. The Social Services Inspectorate has done valuable work in assessing local authorities' regulatory work, but a clear national approach has been lacking.

The current structure of regulation

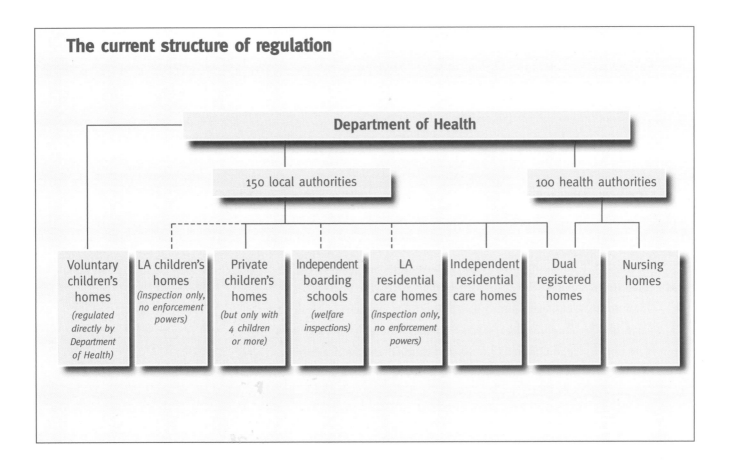

Our plans for reform

4.8 The Government's plans to reform the system of regulation will:

- create Commissions for Care Standards, independent regional authorities responsible solely for the regulation of care services

- introduce new statutory regulation for services not currently covered, including domiciliary care and small children's homes

- improve the way in which registration and inspection are carried out.

4.9 The result should be:

- stronger protection for vulnerable adults and children

- new safeguards for those receiving care at home

- greater assurances that high standards will be met everywhere,
  and greater clarity and consistency for providers as to what
  standards they will be required to meet.

4.10 Our proposals in this Chapter build on Tom Burgner's report,
published in 1996, which followed extensive consultation with all
interested parties, and which set out a strong consensus for change.
They also reflect the recommendations of the Better Regulation Task
Force's report mentioned above.

The Regional Commissions for Care Standards

4.11 To create the new independent structure, we will establish
Commissions for Care Standards (CCSs) at regional level to carry
out the regulation of care services. These will be based on the
boundaries of the NHS and Social Care Regions (see map on
next page), so there will be eight authorities in England.

4.12 The CCSs will be independent statutory bodies, each with their
own Chair and management board. The boards will include
representatives from local authorities and health authorities,
plus user and provider representatives. The Chairs will be
appointed by the Secretary of State.

*'stronger protection
for vulnerable adults
and children'*

*'new independent
Commissions for Care
Standards at regional
level to carry out the
regulation of care
services'*

4.13 The CCSs will have responsibility for regulating the following services:

- residential care homes for adults

- nursing homes

- children's homes

- domiciliary social care providers

- independent fostering agencies

- residential family centres

- boarding schools.

4.14 The CCSs will act in their own right as independent statutory bodies, but will be accountable ultimately to the Secretary of State and to Parliament. There will be arrangements for monitoring the performance of the CCSs and consistency between them from the Department of Health, and the Secretary of State will have powers of direction and guidance over them. There will be recourse to an Ombudsman for complaints against a CCS's exercise of its duties, as well as rights of appeal against deregistration to a Registered Care Tribunal (see paragraph 4.58).

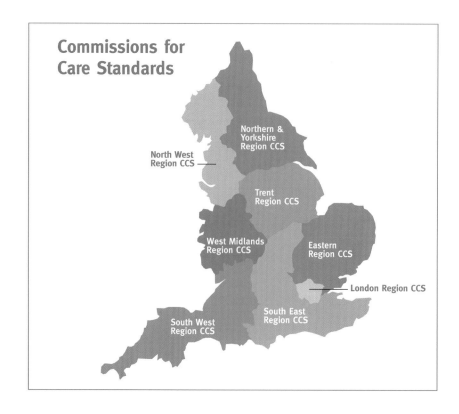

Commissions for Care Standards

4.15 There will be provision for central funding to be granted to the CCSs, but this will not normally need to be used as they will be self-financing through fee income paid by regulated providers. Fee levels will be set by central government for all regulated services.

4.16 Each CCS will have its own workforce of inspectors, and will decide how that workforce should best be deployed, for instance using area offices or teams. The workforce will consist of people with skills and qualifications from both social care and health care, including nurses. The benefits of combining these two sets of skills and backgrounds will best be realised if there is true integrated working, allowing – for instance – nurses to be involved in inspections of children's homes, and social care professionals to be involved in inspecting social aspects of nursing homes. The CCSs will also need good liaison and joint working with other regulatory agencies such as the Health and Safety Executive, fire authorities and environmental health departments.

4.17 It will be important that inspectors should have, and maintain, knowledge of the services that they are inspecting. For many inspectors, the role may be temporary, and it is expected that a spell as an inspector should form part of a professional career path that might also cover working in the commissioning or provision of health or care services. The CCSs will be able to use secondment or other methods such as fixed term or part-time contracts to achieve this.

4.18 The CCSs will also need to have suitable training arrangements for inspectors, and work will be done on developing more uniform methodologies for registration, inspection and enforcement, so that there is greater consistency of practice than at present.

Scope of regulation

Care homes

4.19 Regulation will apply, as now, to residential care homes and nursing homes, although there will be improvements to the way this operates (see paragraph 4.51). In addition, all residential care homes owned by local authorities themselves will be required to register, and will be subject to inspection and enforcement procedures in the same way as will voluntary and private care homes. We will also remove the current exemption for care homes run by organisations established by Royal Charter or Act of Parliament. This is not to say that homes run by such organisations are the subject of particular concern, but the specific exemption for these homes is anomalous, and this is generally accepted among the organisations concerned.

Domiciliary care

4.20 Domiciliary social care is an essential part of good community care. As Chapter 2 makes clear, we want to encourage this as part of our wider aim to promote independence and social inclusion. However, there has never been any statutory system of regulation in domiciliary care, despite the fact that in recent years an increasing proportion of it has been provided by voluntary and private agencies rather than by direct local authority providers.

'we promised in our election manifesto that we would introduce a regulation system for domiciliary care'

4.21 We promised in our election manifesto that we would introduce a regulation system for domiciliary care. Our proposed scheme will offer an assurance of protection to vulnerable users while maintaining the principles of choice and independence that are important to those receiving care.

4.22 The regulation scheme will be based on registering the organisations providing domiciliary care, rather than the individual carers who work in the organisations. The scheme will apply to those organisations who provide personal social care to people living in their own homes. It is not, therefore, intended to cover organisations who provide services of a purely non-care nature, for instance cleaning agencies or gardeners.

4.23 Providers will be registered by the CCS in their area if they demonstrate that they meet the required criteria and standards. These will need to be developed, but they are likely to cover areas such as:

- fitness of owner and manager

- personnel issues (including recruitment/vetting procedures, personnel records, policies on training, health and safety, equal opportunities etc.)

- information to users (e.g. on charges, service withdrawals, how to complain etc.)

- quality procedures (including complaints procedures, systems for monitoring user satisfaction, supervision of care staff etc.)

- operational policies (e.g. administration of medicines, confidentiality, health and safety, promotion of choice, access to users' homes etc.)

- financial viability and insurance.

4.24 The standards will be developed in consultation with interested parties, and will be set at national level in the same way as for other services (see paragraph 4.46 below).

4.25 As with care homes, local authority home care services will be registered, inspected and subject to enforcement action in the same way as independent providers. Registration requirements will be uniform, regardless of whether the organisation is private, voluntary or statutory, and whether it is a "principal" organisation or an agency. Arrangements will be made to ensure that there is no unnecessary duplication, for example when several branches of the same organisation are to be registered.

4.26 Once a provider organisation is registered, it will be subject to annual review by the CCS, and may also be inspected at any time. Inspection may involve a variety of methods, such as scrutiny of records, interviews with staff and sample interviews with users, in order to check whether registration standards continue to be met.

'providers will be registered by the CCS in their area if they demonstrate that they meet the required criteria and standards'

'registration requirements will be uniform, regardless of whether the organisation is private, voluntary or statutory, and whether it is a "principal" organisation or an agency'

4.27 If a registered provider is in breach of one or more of the registration requirements, the CCS will have powers to serve enforcement notices, and ultimately to deregister. In cases of deregistration, the provider will have right of appeal to the Registered Care Tribunal (see paragraph 4.58).

4.28 Registration will not be compulsory for all providers, although it is expected that the great majority will wish to be registered. However, local authorities will be required, when making arrangements for domiciliary care under their community care responsibilities, to place contracts only with registered domiciliary care providers.

'the Government's intention is not to remove all responsibility from individuals in making choices about their own care, but to offer the assurance of protection to everyone who wishes to take advantage of it'

4.29 The CCSs will be able to provide published lists of registered providers to any individuals who wish to make their own privately-purchased care arrangements. We will not, however, prohibit private individuals from making their own care arrangements with relatives, friends or others who are not registered care providers, if they choose to do so. The Government's intention is not to remove all responsibility from individuals in making choices about their own care, but to offer the assurance of protection to everyone who wishes to take advantage of it. It will be important for the CCSs to publicise widely the fact that a domiciliary care registration scheme exists, to ensure that everyone who wishes to use a registered provider can do so.

4.30 We believe that this scheme of regulation will provide a real assurance of protection to users, and will be workable. The introduction of the scheme will represent a substantial amount of work for the CCSs in their first few years. Once the system has bedded down, we intend that there should be a review of the operation of the scheme to see whether further improvements need to be made.

Children's services

4.31 The Government has recently published its response to the Children's Safeguards Review (see Chapter 3). That response included commitments to improve the regulatory arrangements for children living away from home. These regulatory responsibilities will fall to the new CCSs when established.

4.32 There are currently different regulation arrangements for different types of children's homes (see chart after 4.7). In future, all children's homes will be registered and inspected by the CCSs. The additional Secretary of State approval that is required for homes used as secure accommodation will remain.

'in future, all children's homes will be registered and inspected by the CCSs'

4.33 The regulation of children's day care is not covered in this Chapter. The Government published a consultation document in March 1998 on the future arrangements for the regulation of under-eights services, including day care, and of early education providers. This is in line with the Government's manifesto commitment to review the currently separate regulatory systems in these two sectors. The Government will be considering the options in the light of the responses to consultation and the plans set out in this White Paper.

Voluntary children's homes

4.34 At present, the 60 or so voluntary children's homes in England are registered and inspected by the Department of Health directly, while all other homes are registered and inspected by local authorities. In recent years, a number of inquiries and reviews have recommended that voluntary children's homes should be regulated in the same way as all other children's homes, and we support this view. The CCSs will therefore have the responsibility for registering and inspecting voluntary children's homes.

Small private children's homes

4.35 Private children's homes with fewer than four children are currently not required to be registered. The Government considers this unacceptable, and agrees with the recommendation of (among others) the Burgner Report and the Children's Safeguards Review, that these homes must be regulated. We will therefore require small private children's homes to be registered and inspected by the CCSs.

4.36 The same regulatory system will in principle apply to all children's homes, whether private, voluntary or local authority, and – as far as possible – whatever the size. Regulation should not be more burdensome than is necessary, but the first priority must be to safeguard children. All homes will be subject to mandatory inspection.

Residential family centres

'the Government also intends to introduce regulation for residential family centres operated by local authorities or independent providers'

4.37 The Government also intends to introduce regulation for residential family centres operated by local authorities or independent providers. These centres have not been subject to any regulation, because children remain in the care of their parent(s) while in the centre. The Government considers that appropriate regulation should apply to these centres. We intend that mother and baby homes – currently regulated as nursing homes – should in future be subject to the same regulation as residential family centres. The CCSs will carry out the regulation responsibilities.

Independent fostering agencies

4.38 Most children who are looked after by foster parents are in placements provided and managed by local authority social services. However, the Children Act permits local authorities to delegate certain of their fostering duties to voluntary organisations, and over the last few years there has been a growth of these independent fostering agencies. In line with the recommendations from the Burgner Report and the Children's Safeguards Review, we plan to bring independent fostering agencies within the regulatory framework, and they too will be regulated by the CCSs. We intend to allow private as well as voluntary organisations to act as fostering agencies, as long as they meet the standards of the regulation system.

4.39 The Burgner Report also suggested that the regulation requirements for independent fostering agencies should be extended to local authority fostering services, to ensure even-handedness for such services. We plan to require local authority fostering services to meet the same standards as the independent fostering agencies.

Welfare inspection of boarding schools

4.40 Inspections of the welfare arrangements for children accommodated in boarding schools currently apply to independent schools only (under Section 87 of the Children Act). The Children's Safeguards Review recommended that the duty on independent boarding schools to safeguard and promote the welfare of children they accommodate, should be extended to all schools with boarding provision. These include all LEA maintained boarding schools, and special schools approved to take children with special educational needs. We will extend welfare inspections to these other types of schools. The responsibility for all welfare inspections of schools with boarding provision will transfer from local authorities to the CCSs.

'we plan to bring independent fostering agencies within the regulatory framework'

Regional children's rights officers

'Children's Rights Officers for each region'

4.41 The Government wants to ensure that children's welfare is given the highest priority by the CCSs – the regulation of children's services must not be swamped by the much larger volume of adult services that the Commissions will deal with. We intend to establish arrangements for a nominated high-level officer to take charge of the children's regulatory function in each CCS.

4.42 The Government is anxious that this new development should also provide a channel of communication for serious concerns relating to children's safety and rights. We intend therefore to designate the senior officer referred to above as the Children's Rights Officer for the regional area covered by the CCS. The role of that officer, subject to the CCS itself and to guidance and direction that the Secretary of State may issue, will be to:

- help the CCS to give a full and effective coverage of children's services and children's rights in their statutory regulatory responsibilities and in the reports they make on the discharge of those responsibilities

- ensure that the views of children placed in the facilities and services regulated by the CCS are given proper weight in that regulatory task. This will include close liaison with the new arrangements for promoting the voice of the child in care described in Chapter 3

- report directly to the Chief Inspector of the Social Services Inspectorate any significant evidence relevant to the rights and safety of children gained from the CCS's regulation and assessment of services for children, which might help local authorities or other providers to improve the services and support they give to children.

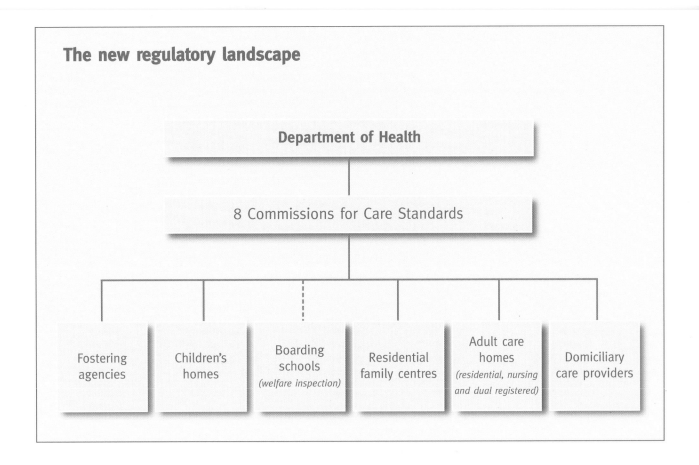

The new regulatory landscape

Department of Health

8 Commissions for Care Standards

| Fostering agencies | Children's homes | Boarding schools *(welfare inspection)* | Residential family centres | Adult care homes *(residential, nursing and dual registered)* | Domiciliary care providers |

Other services

4.43 The Government does not intend at this stage to introduce new regulation for other service areas, such as day care for adults or field social work. The need for regulation in these and any other areas will be reviewed from time to time, but the Government's aim is that the new CCSs, once established, must concentrate on carrying out effectively the regulatory duties given to them. In due time, as patterns of services change, there may be a need for changes in the range of services subject to regulation. We intend that the legislative framework for the new regulation system should allow for flexibility and adaptation in response to such changes.

'the legislative framework for the new regulation system should allow for flexibility and adaptation'

4.44 The Government is considering how best to deal with the regulation of the independent acute health sector which is currently regulated on the same basis as nursing homes. In the same context it will look at the most appropriate arrangements for regulating independent mental health hospitals. It will also be considering further the regulation of nurses' agencies, particularly in view of the introduction of regulation for domiciliary care, to see what improvements can be made to the current system.

Other improvements to the regulation system

4.45 As well as the structural changes outlined above, we intend to improve the way in which regulation is carried out.

More consistent standards

4.46 Currently the Registered Homes Act and its regulations do not set out much detail in terms of the standards that care homes must meet. The Children Act is more prescriptive about the standards for children's homes, but essentially a great deal of discretion is left to the individual local authorities and health authorities in setting standards. Although local discretion allows flexibility, it means that there is inconsistency between authorities, leaving providers uncertain about what they need to do in order to be registered, and leaving service users unclear about what standards they can expect as a minimum in all care homes. The Government is therefore committed to introducing a greater degree of consistency in regulation standards.

4.47 The introduction of the new CCSs provides the organisational basis for more consistency in regulation, as well as reducing duplicated bureaucracy. Where there are currently 250 registering authorities, there will in future be eight. The Government will also develop national regulatory standards to be applied consistently by all eight CCSs.

4.48 There is always a tension between national prescription and local discretion, and too much national prescription can lead to bad regulation. The key objective must be to develop a limited range of standards to apply at national level, with a certain degree of flexibility allowed more locally. These standards will focus on the key areas that most affect the quality of life experienced by service users, as well as physical standards. The regulatory standards will need to have regard to costs and effectiveness when they are being developed.

'a limited range of standards to apply at national level, with a certain degree of flexibility allowed more locally'

4.49 Overall, there will be three levels at which standards are set:

- some standards will be set firmly in legislation, and these will be non-negotiable (an example in the current system is the requirement that the person in charge of a nursing home must be a registered nurse or medical practitioner)

- some standards will be spelled out at national level (for example, required procedures for the proper selection and vetting of staff)

- some of these standards will allow for interpretation by the CCSs, who will be able to define their own requirements within the limits of the national standards (for example, timescales within which specific below-standard accomodation must be upgraded).

4.50 The standards for all the various regulated services will be developed through a consultative process. As a first step, the Government has commissioned the Centre for Policy on Ageing to advise on proposed national standards for the largest group of regulated services, residential and nursing home care for older people. The outcome of this project which will be the subject of consultation will provide a basis for developing standards in other areas.

'standards for all the various regulated services will be developed through a consultative process'

Greater flexibilities in residential and nursing home care

4.51 The Registered Homes Act 1984 introduced, for the first time, the provision for a single home to be registered to provide both residential care and nursing care. In theory, this would allow much greater flexibility, with residents allowed to remain in the same home when their condition requires a greater level of care. However, it meant that homes had to register separately with two different authorities (the local authority and the health authority), who might have different standards and procedures. In practice dual registration has proved too bureaucratic and time-consuming for many homeowners, and for the health and local authorities.

4.52 The benefits of one home being able to cater for a wide range of needs are clear, for social services, for providers, and most importantly for users, who can feel more assured of having a "home for life" if that is what they wish. The Government wishes to encourage this type of provision, although it is for homeowners themselves to decide what services they wish to offer, and many will of course wish to specialise in particular needs.

4.53 The new CCSs will bring together the currently separate regulation responsibilities for residential care homes and nursing homes. In addition, the national standards that are developed for residential and nursing home care will take an integrated approach, with common standards for all care homes, differing only in matters related to the nursing care needs of those in nursing homes. It should therefore be no more difficult for a provider to register to provide both residential and nursing care, than it is to register to provide either one or the other. In this way, we hope to introduce the greatest level of flexibility while retaining the protections that are necessary. In due course, it may be sensible to move to a single registration category for all care homes, and we intend that the legislative framework should be flexible enough to allow this possibility.

Inspection

4.54 As mentioned above, the new CCSs will have the responsibility to deploy staff appropriately to carry out inspection work, and there will be a more consistent approach to methodologies of inspection and related activities. Inspections – particularly unannounced inspections – are an important method for checking that vulnerable people are receiving the protection and care that they require. They will remain an essential part of regulation. The Government believes that greater use could be made of risk assessment procedures in order to ensure that greater attention is paid to providers where risks to users appear to be greater. This would mean that providers would be assessed in relation to various factors, including past history, previous concerns or complaints, and other matters. Other quality assurance mechanisms – such as independent accreditation schemes – could also be taken into account in determining the level of attention paid to a particular provider. All providers will nevertheless have a minimum frequency of inspections. For care homes this will remain at two per year.

4.55 The current lack of mandatory inspections for adult homes with fewer than four residents is no longer acceptable. Currently there is no requirement to inspect, and guidance issued under the previous administration actively discouraged authorities from inspecting such homes. The Government accepts that small homes, because of their domestic nature, should not be required to meet regulation standards that would undermine their very purpose. The national regulatory standards will take account of this. However, in order to ensure that vulnerable people receive the protection they deserve, we will introduce a requirement that all such homes should be inspected at least once per year. In addition, the definition of small homes will be tightened up to make clear that they are those which are genuinely in small-scale domestic settings.

'greater use could be made of risk assessment procedures'

Complaints, enforcement and appeals

4.56 Effective and easily accessible complaints procedures are an important part of ensuring that care provision continues to meet the necessary standards. The recent Office of Fair Trading inquiry into care homes found evidence of confusion and variation in what complaints procedures were available and how well they were understood. We will be undertaking further work to tackle this issue and to ensure that complaints procedures are better publicised and understood by service users and carers. We will also consider in establishing the CCSs how best to ensure complementarity and coherence between the various complaints procedures that apply to care homes and other regulated services.

'a greater degree of consistency in enforcement practice'

4.57 All services subject to regulation will be subject to appropriate enforcement action. This will include powers to serve improvement notices, to prosecute, and where necessary to deregister, including emergency closure. We aim to achieve a greater degree of consistency in enforcement practice under the new system, so that people can be assured that action will be taken to improve standards and – where necessary – to close down services. CCSs will act in accordance with the Government's Enforcement Concordat.

4.58 Providers will have rights of appeal against deregistration decisions, and formal appeals will be made to a national independent tribunal. This will in future be called the Registered Care Tribunal, and will replace the current Registered Homes Tribunal. As well as making the necessary changes to the Tribunal to allow it to consider appeals for new services (for instance, domiciliary care providers and independent fostering agencies), we will take the opportunity to make changes to improve its operations. There is a need to cut down the delays that can occur in Tribunal cases, and we will shortly be taking steps to improve this through changes to the Tribunal's procedures. But there are other problems with the Tribunal, for instance a high percentage of appeals that are withdrawn (sometimes at the last minute), and a tendency for cases to be over-legalistic.

We will consult with interested parties, including the Council on Tribunals, when drawing up plans for establishing the Registered Care Tribunal to ensure that it provides, as originally intended, a speedy, inexpensive and simple means of resolving disputes without recourse to the Courts. This is in everyone's interest, not least the service users who can suffer most from delays in the current system.

Conclusion

4.59 Our proposals for improving the way services are regulated will provide better protection for vulnerable people, as well as giving providers a clearer and more efficient system to work with.

4.60 The majority of our plans will need primary legislation, and we intend to legislate as soon as Parliamentary time is available to implement them. We will continue to work with all interested parties as we move to making our proposals reality. As part of this, we will assess closely the costs and benefits of our proposals, as with all proposed regulatory measures. We have produced a draft regulatory impact appraisal, which will be developed as we move to legislation. The draft appraisal is available from the contact point at the end of this White Paper.

4.61 In the meantime, local authorities and health authorities remain responsible for regulation under existing legislation. It is essential that those responsibilities are conscientiously carried out, and the Government will not tolerate any cutting back of activity or resources in this area by authorities because it is a responsibility they are about to lose. Protection of vulnerable people is essential now as well as in the future. We will be ensuring that regulation is a priority area for authorities in the period before the new system is established. The National Priorities Guidance gives effect to this by specifically identifying regulation as one of the priorities for both health and social services.

'regulation is a priority area for authorities in the period before the new system is established'

5

Key themes

- *raising standards in social care staff: the General Social Care Council*
- *a national training strategy*

Improving standards in the workforce

creating a General Social Care Council, improving training

Introduction

'people who work in social care are called on to respond to some of the most demanding, often distressing and intractable human problems'

5.1 Social care has been one of the fastest growing employment sectors in recent years, and the workforce now numbers around one million. This includes people working in a wide range of care settings, two thirds of them in the independent sector (mainly working in residential homes).

5.2 The people who work in social care are called on to respond to some of the most demanding, often distressing and intractable human problems. Yet there are few public accolades for getting it right and virulent criticism for getting it wrong. Staff can feel embattled and undervalued, and their morale suffers.

5.3 The Government recognises this, and has no wish to undermine or attack those who work in the social care sector. Nevertheless, there are serious problems which we will tackle:

- 80% of this large workforce which works directly with very vulnerable people have no recognised qualifications or training

- there are no national mechanisms to set and enforce standards of practice and conduct. Health care professions have had such mechanisms for many years. A General Teaching Council has just been established. Yet for social workers and other social care staff there has been no comparable body, even though they often have access to people's confidential and intimate lives

- the standards and suitability of some education and training in social care do not enjoy general confidence.

5.4 A competent and confident workforce is an essential component of the modernisation of social services. The policy agenda and explicit service objectives set out in this White Paper have profound implications for the workforce, not only the 40,000 or so professionally qualified social workers, but also the much larger number of care staff providing the bulk of the day to day care. All the staff need to play their part in moving social work away from the public perception of an association with dependence to the promotion of independence, and achieving the provision of safer services for children and modern, enabling services for adults.

5.5 To give their best, staff will need support by:

- clear definition by employers of their roles and the way they are deployed

- individual objectives related to service objectives

- better supervision and management

- improved education and training which is geared to the new agenda.

5.6 In this context the Government judges that institutional change is essential to improve standards and public confidence and to give those working in social care a new status which fits the work they do. It will therefore:

- introduce legislation when Parliamentary time allows, to create a new General Social Care Council which will replace the Central Council for Education and Training in Social Work in regulating the training of social workers; set conduct and practice standards for all social services staff; and register those in the most sensitive areas

- develop a new training strategy centred around a new National Training Organisation for social care staff.

'to give those working in social care a new status which fits the work they do'

'a new statutory body called the General Social Care Council'

5.7 The Government believes that the need to improve public protection, to raise the quality of services and improve performance, and to give proper recognition to the vocational commitment of the workforce, requires the regulatory framework for social care to be strengthened by regulating social care personnel for the first time. To do this it will create a new statutory body called the General Social Care Council.

Governance issues

5.8 The constitution of the GSCC, its methods of operation and the arrangements for its governance will reflect a paramount general duty to secure the interests and the welfare of service users and the confidence of the public. It will be an independent statutory body with clear functions which it will be responsible for discharging efficiently and effectively. The proper discharge of the functions are however a matter of some importance to the Government and the wider public. The Council will therefore be appointed by the Secretary of State and be accountable to him for the way it performs. It will also operate generally with the approval and consent of the Secretary of State and subject to such guidance or directions as he may give. We also intend that the Secretary of State should have powers of default.

5.9 The Government intends the GSCC to be lean and effective. It will be only as big as is needed to secure the cost-effective discharge of its business and is unlikely to exceed 25 people. The Council will need to be able to employ staff for its day-to-day work, with the approval of the Secretary of State. It is intended that the directly employed staff of the Council will be as small as possible with full use made of bought-in skills.

5.10 In keeping with its objectives the Council will be composed of people representing all the key interests. It will be chaired by a lay person appointed by the Secretary of State and half the members will be appointed so that service users and lay members will be a majority of the Council. Appointments will be made after consultation with service user interests and by inviting applications from the public.

5.11 The remaining members will be drawn from employment, professional and education interests including local government, independent sector employers, and social services education and training. The various representative bodies in these fields will be invited to suggest nominations for appointment of people who can bring the necessary skills and knowledge the Council will need to do its job.

5.12 It will be necessary for the GSCC to discharge its functions through properly constituted committees. The Government will provide for powers to create such committees by approval of the Secretary of State.

5.13 Broadly, the Government intends that any start-up costs and the costs of the regulation of professional social work training will be met at an appropriate level from sums currently allocated to the Central Council for Education and Training in Social Work. The Government believes that registered staff should pay a fee to meet the registration costs and expects that this will be a sum similar to that payable by nurses to the United Kingdom Central Council for Nursing, Midwifery and Health Visiting (UKCC). It therefore intends that the Council, when established, should have powers to receive central grants and to levy registration fees set with the approval of the Secretary of State. The Council will similarly have powers to raise income from charging for any services provided to employers, awarding bodies and educational institutions.

Objectives of the GSCC

5.14 The Government believes that the GSCC must be designed to meet the particular needs of modern social care and the aspirations of the public. The social care workforce is not a homogeneous group of professionally qualified staff. It is large, the people are employed in a diverse range of settings where expectations vary, and they are largely unqualified. Neither is there a generally accepted and widely understood set of values and ethics or standards of conduct and practice which is reflected in the attitudes of the staff as a whole.

'the GSCC must meet the particular needs of modern social care and the aspirations of the public'

5.15 Against this background the Government believes that the GSCC should deliver two key objectives. These are:

- to strengthen public protection by relevant and appropriate regulation of personnel which has the interests of service users and the public at its heart

- to ensure through a coherent, well developed and regulated training system that more staff are equipped to provide social care which allows and assists individuals to live their own lives, and offers practical help, based on research and other evidence of what works, and free of unnecessary ideological influences.

Setting the standards

'consistent action must now be taken to set enforceable standards of conduct and practice'

5.16 The Government recognises that the majority of staff carry out their work safely and with humanity often in situations of great difficulty. The Government believes that consistent action must now be taken to set enforceable standards of conduct and practice for the whole workforce and that these standards should be published in codes. Codes will enable users and the public to know what standards they can expect of staff. They will also guide all staff and their employers in a common understanding of conduct and practice requirements. The Government therefore intends the GSCC to have the necessary powers to set standards and that drawing up the codes will be the first priority for the Council.

5.17 Individual practitioners should be personally accountable for their own standards of conduct and practice based on the codes. They will therefore be required to sign up to the codes as a condition of their employment. However, service users and the public must have satisfactory assurance that where conduct and practice fall short of the accepted standard, effective action to enforce the codes can be taken, and where necessary, unsuitable individuals removed from the workforce. The Government intends to achieve this by reinforcing the responsibilities of employers to adopt and rigorously apply the best employment practices when recruiting people and when taking disciplinary action against unsatisfactory members of staff.

5.18 The GSCC will therefore also draw up and promulgate a code of practice for employers. This will be enforced even-handedly in the regulated services by the Commissions for Care Standards (described in the previous Chapter) through the national regulatory standards. Where necessary the code will be enforced in the statutory sector using the existing powers of direction and guidance given to the Secretary of State.

Registration of individuals

5.19 Most regulatory bodies use registers in some form as a way of setting and maintaining standards for entry to and remaining in the professional or occupational group concerned. The Government accepts that registration of individuals has a part to play in improving the quality of the staff and in strengthening public protection. It therefore intends that the GSCC will have a registration function. However, the Government believes that existing models of regulation used in other areas are not appropriate for social care and the circumstances of the workforce described earlier. The registration function of the GSCC will be framed specifically and introduced incrementally to secure the best interests of service users and the public.

> *'registration of individuals has a part to play'*

5.20 Registration can strengthen the regulatory framework and public protection only if it has a proper basis. The Government does not accept it is sensible to proceed at once with registration of a largely unqualified workforce on the basis of vetting procedures alone. With a workforce of a million, this would be costly and cumbersome, and would not in practice lead to better standards. The Government has therefore decided that registration by the GSCC will be based on the satisfactory completion of approved training which provides the necessary skills and knowledge for safe, effective and lawful practice in any job or at any level. The Secretary of State will approve the opening of a register where, in his opinion, a registration requirement would justify the cost by reliably adding to the safeguards to the public; and when he can accept advice from the GSCC that for the relevant section of the workforce the following conditions are met:

- a suitable form of training exists

- an education/training supply side is capable of delivering that training

- a large enough proportion of the people in the group concerned have completed the training to make the register viable.

'considerable improvements in the levels of training and qualifications'

5.21 The criteria for registration are already met in respect of qualified social work staff. The GSCC will therefore be able soon after its establishment to open a register of people who have obtained a professional social work qualification. The GSCC will however be concerned with the whole workforce, and the Government wants to see considerable improvements in the levels of training and qualifications generally. It sees the GSCC as playing a significant role in achieving that objective.

5.22 It therefore intends that another group of staff will be registered at or about the time of the professionally qualified staff. The Government has already provided £2 million for 1998/99 in its Training Support Programme to enable residential child care workers to be qualified at NVQ Level 3. The Government expects that this group of staff will be registered as well as social workers.

5.23 Taking this priority approach to training and subsequent registration, the Government has identified heads of care homes as a group in which it expects to see more progress in the next few years. Most heads of children's homes have already been qualified to Diploma in Social Work level, and will therefore be eligible for registration on that basis. However, only a relatively small percentage of heads of adult care homes are similarly qualified. The Government wishes to see more heads of homes, particularly in the adult care sector, appropriately qualified. It will be working with the sector to ensure that suitable training which can build on the considerable experience of many heads of homes is put in place. The Government can then consider whether registration of heads of homes with the GSCC would be a helpful further step.

5.24 It is common in other professions for continued registration to be linked to continuing professional education and development. The Government believes that while individual workers have a personal responsibility to ensure they are up to date, more positive steps are needed. It therefore intends to provide for periodic re-registration to be introduced when the Secretary of State considers it appropriate.

Deregistration

5.25 The GSCC will have the power to deregister individuals for breach of the codes of conduct and practice. The Government intends that the deregistration mechanism which may provide for hearings to determine the facts and adjudicate the matter will operate so as to ensure that proper weight is given to the interests of the service users concerned. Provision will also be made for immediate suspension from the register in appropriate cases prior to the full hearing of the issues.

5.26 As set out in Chapter 3, the Government intends to strengthen the Consultancy Index which includes the names of persons who are considered unsuitable to work with children. The Government will ensure that the GSCC and the new Consultancy Index complement each other.

'the GSCC will have the power to deregister individuals for breach of the codes of conduct and practice'

Job reservation

5.27 In some professions or occupational groups it is common for restrictions to apply which allow only registered staff to carry out certain work. For instance, only a nurse registered with the UKCC may work as a nurse in the NHS. The Government does not think that such a blanket approach is possible or even desirable in social care. Social care is increasingly multi-disciplinary in nature involving the medical, nursing and other professions allied to medicine, for example. Developments in delivering social care and restructuring in local government are also continuing to break down traditional roles or functions which are in any case very difficult to define. The Government does not wish to stifle such developments by building rigidities into the regulatory system. The Government therefore sees no case for general job reservation.

5.28 But it will be considering the circumstances in which the public interest requires a statutory restriction on employment. In some areas, there are existing statutory restrictions which effectively result in job reservation. The Mental Health Act 1983 requires that certain mental health functions are carried out by Approved Social Workers (qualified social workers who have completed a further course of specialist training). In the case of registered nursing homes there is a regulatory requirement for heads of homes to be registered nurses or medical practitioners. The Government believes that for heads of other types of homes there is a case to be considered for restricting these posts to people with particular qualifications. This could be done through the statutory basis for regulation of these services at some future date when this part of the workforce can be and is trained to an appropriate level as described above.

5.29 There is also a strong case for ensuring that some areas of children's services involving highly specialised functions such as management of children's cases involving the exercise of statutory powers, child protection, and assessing families with particularly complex needs, should be restricted to individuals who are registered by the GSCC or the statutory regulatory bodies for the health professions. The Government will be considering this area further and will seek an appropriate power to introduce job reservation when the Secretary of State considers it to be right. The Government will, however, use such a power cautiously and selectively so that it does not block the involvement of a range of professional and occupational skills.

Regulation of education and training

'*CCETSW will be abolished*'

5.30 The Government has already announced that when the GSCC is established, it will take on responsibility for the regulation of professional social work training from the Central Council for Education and Training in Social Work which will then be abolished. It will also be the statutory body responsible for advising the Secretary of State on the suitability and cost effectiveness of training across the social care workforce prior to the establishment of registers. It will, therefore, take a keen interest in the availability and "fitness for purpose" of training.

5.31 It will be important for the GSCC to establish and maintain close links with the National Training Organisation (see paragraph 5.34), the Qualifications and Curriculum Authority and awarding bodies for NVQ level training to ensure that occupational standards, course content, assessment arrangements and programme approval mechanisms produce qualifications of a quality and consistency on which registration can be based.

5.32 The Government intends the GSCC to have the powers necessary to reshape and maintain the professional training system to ensure that it is fit for purpose. As in other professions, it is important that professionally qualified social workers base their practice on the best evidence of what works for clients and are responsive to new ideas from research. Their early education and training will play a significant part in encouraging a flexible, intelligent approach to practice in later years and assist social workers in taking personal responsibility for their continuing professional education and development. The Government believes that the regulation of the training system must also be responsive to the changing needs of the services and their users. It will expect, facilitate and encourage all key interests – users, the public and employers – to see that this happens.

'it is important that professionally qualified social workers base their practice on the best evidence of what works for clients'

5.33 It will therefore be an early priority of the GSCC to consider and take what action is necessary to redefine the regulation of professional social work training. This is however an area to which the Government has attached such importance that it has put in place a programme of work to secure some improvements in the system in advance of and for the benefit of the new Council. Much of this work will be done in conjunction with employment and academic interests.

A training strategy

5.34 Alongside the GSCC's role in setting the standards for training in social care, the development and promotion of training at all levels will be the main responsibility of the recently licensed Training Organisation for Personal Social Services. This national training organisation (NTO), like those for other industries, is an employment-led body representing the whole sector, including service users. Its functions are:

'a new National Training Organisation'

- to maintain the occupational standards underpinning the qualifications recognised by social care staff and employers

- to carry out workforce analysis

- to identify training needs and ensure they are met.

5.35 The new NTO provides a unique opportunity to capitalise on and unite past work in the areas of training and workforce analysis. In recent years our understanding of the characteristics and dynamics of the social services workforce, and the priority areas for improvements in education and training, has increased significantly. Research funded by the Department of Health has played an important part in establishing the sound knowledge base required to underpin plans for future investment in the workforce, and we intend that high quality research shall continue to play an important role. However, more is needed than mere consolidation and further analysis. The Government believes there is a need to put in place a training strategy for social care which defines a new and more effective agenda. This does not have to wait for the establishment of the GSCC, and as a start, the Government has, jointly with the NTO, held a conference of all the major interests in social care to begin addressing: the key elements of a training strategy in social care; the need for clear agreements linking staff groups to the training and qualifications structure; targets for quantitative and qualitative improvements; the commitment of all employers to their achievement; and the key role of the NTO in delivering results.

5.36 The co-operative development of a national training strategy for social care does not diminish the continuing responsibilities of all employers for wider workforce issues and for linking these to local corporate objectives. The Government wishes to see further developments of local human resource strategies, of which training is one part, which are themselves more comprehensively connected to coherent business and training plans. With a large, diverse workforce it is essential that employers have a clear sense of their workforce, have carefully analysed the sorts of skills and people they need to achieve their business objectives, and can plan and direct the available resources for training to where they are needed.

Training support programme

5.37 The Training Support Programme (TSP) is a central programme supported by the Training Support Grant. The Government will provide from the Social Services Modernisation Fund an extra £19.7 million for the Training Support Grant over the next three years. The Government intends that in future this money will be increasingly geared towards raising qualification levels. Once the NTO has mapped the workforce and achieved some consensus in qualifications linked to particular occupational groups, it will be possible to set qualification targets for these groups. The Training Support Grant will be used to support the achievement of these targets.

5.38 Given the priority of improving services for children, the Government has already put in place a range of new child care training initiatives which will receive funding from the TSP. They include:

- £1 million rising to £6 million over three years to enable 7,000 social workers engaged in child care and child protection work to achieve a new post-qualifying award

- £2.5 million rising to £3m over three years for 9,500 residential child care workers to attain an NVQ level 3.

5.39 There will in addition be about £500,000 available for each of the next three years for training top social services managers, which will also help to implement the Quality Protects programme.

Conclusion

5.40 Good social services cannot be delivered without good staff. Work in the social care field is an important vocation through which many people give valuable service to individuals and the community. To give greater public recognition of this, the Government intends to introduce an awards scheme for outstanding individual social care staff, beginning next year. Through improvements in training arrangements, and through the work of the GSCC, we intend to ensure that the social care workforce is fit for delivering modern, high quality services, and that all the people who work in social care can feel that their work and their commitment are given the recognition that they deserve.

'the Government will provide an extra £19.7 million for the Training Support Grant over the next three years'

'through improvements in training arrangements, and through the work of the GSCC, we intend to ensure that the social care workforce is fit for delivering modern, high quality services'

6

Key themes

- *better joint working to help people get the services they need*
- *integrated health and social care*
- *better co-ordination of children's services*

Improving partnerships

better joint working for more effective services

Introduction

6.1 An important feature of the provision of social services is that social services are rarely the only public service in contact with a family or individual service user. The main agencies who work alongside social services include:

- the National Health Service

- local housing departments

- the employment service

- the education service

- the criminal justice system.

6.2 As well as these statutory agencies, social services operate more broadly in partnerships with voluntary organisations, independent providers and with users, their carers and their representatives. This Chapter sets out action to help social services to work in effective partnerships in the best interests of service users.

6.3 Although there are often difficulties in bringing together different agencies' responsibilities, major reorganisation of service boundaries – always a tempting solution – does not provide the answer. This would simply create new boundaries and lead to instability and diversion of management effort. Instead, the Government is fostering a new spirit of flexible partnership working which moves away from sterile conflicts over boundaries to an approach where this wasted time and effort is directed positively towards working across them. The Government will play its part in helping this partnership approach by removing legal and other obstacles to joint working, and by adopting the same principles of partnership and joint working in policy-making as we expect from those who are responsible for delivering the services at local level.

6.4 The Government's reforms to modernise local government, set out in the White Paper *Modern Local Government: In Touch with the People,* will place on local authorities clearer duties to act corporately in the interests of their local citizens, and they will need to forge partnerships with other services to carry out those duties.

'flexible partnership working which moves away from sterile conflicts over boundaries'

Partnership with the NHS

6.5 The National Health Service is a crucial partner in almost all social services work. This is particularly true in services for elderly people, people with mental health problems, people with physical disability or a learning disability, and some children's services. The Government has made it one of its top priorities since coming to office to bring down the "Berlin Wall" that can divide health and social services, and to create a system of integrated care that puts users at the centre of service provision. People do not fit into neat service categories, and if partner agencies are not working together it is the user who suffers.

New corporate duties of local authorities

The White Paper *Modern Local Government: In Touch with the People* set out a new legal duty which will be placed on local authorities to "promote the economic, environmental and social well-being of all their citizens". The intention is that authorities should stop thinking in terms of discrete, departmental functions, and start thinking more corporately about what will benefit their citizens, cutting across traditional service boundaries if need be. This will require close partnership working both within authorities (for instance, between social services and education) and with other agencies (such as the police and the NHS).

6.6 Both health and social services authorities recognise this and many have worked hard to develop means of joint working to enable users to receive the high quality, integrated services they need.

6.7 We know that there is plenty of enthusiasm among staff and managers in health and social services to work together innovatively. We saw the benefits of this in the use of the extra funding provided to cope with 1997/98 winter pressures (see box). That is why we are continuing this winter pressures money for a second year. And there have been many excellent examples of joint working in other areas, for example in child and adolescent mental health services.

6.8 But we need to translate these individual examples of good practice into routine joint working at all levels and in all parts of the country. We are determined to overcome the obstacles to effective joint working that remain.

Good practice in joint working: use of winter pressures money

An extra £159 million was made available during the 1997/98 winter period to help ease pressure on the health and social care system. Elderly people are particularly vulnerable during the winter months, and all too often, an emergency admission to hospital following a fall or other problem becomes a permanent stay either in hospital or a care home. Increased admissions of older people puts pressure on the whole hospital system, creating difficulties in dealing with other emergency cases. The extra money was used in many areas to tackle this problem, for example:

In **Lambeth, Southwark** and **Lewisham,** the local hospitals appointed discharge co-ordinators to work closely with the three local social services departments to ensure that people could return to their own homes – with support – at the earliest opportunity.

In **Bromley,** the continuing care multi-disciplinary team provided intensive medical, nursing and therapy care for patients in their own home – without this service half of the 135 patients dealt with by the team would have been referred directly to hospital for admission.

In **Greenwich,** additional funding was used to enhance the provision of community alarms. 93 new alarms were provided during the winter of which 85% were connected within 48 hours. The average age of recipients was 78.

Additional funding of £209 million for England was announced for winter pressures in 1998/99, and this will fund further joint health and social care initiatives around the country.

6.9 Some of the Government's initiatives to improve joint working between health and social services have been mentioned in Chapter 2. They include the Better Services for Vulnerable People initiative, the new Promoting Independence grants which encourage joint

working, the Long-term Care Charter, and the development of
National Service Frameworks covering both health and social care.

6.10 We will also be legislating to make joint working easier. The
proposals in our consultation document *Partnership in action*
include new arrangements to allow health and social services
authorities to work together better (see box). These flexible
approaches will benefit services for all population groups:
children, young people, working age adults and elderly people.

'legislative change to make joint working easier'

Partnership in action – the Government's proposals

The Government will legislate to make it easier for health and social services authorities to work together. The three key proposals are:

• **pooled budgets** – where health and social services put a proportion of their funds into a mutually accessible joint budget to enable more integrated care. Pooled budgets will require robust management and accountability arrangements

• **lead commissioning** – where one authority transfers funds to the other who will then take responsibility for purchasing both health and social care. The legislation will allow the local authority or health authority to delegate their functions and money

• **integrated provision** – where one organisation provides both health and social care. It is often integrated provision (for example of health and social care for learning disabled people) which brings most immediate benefit to users. This flexibility would allow NHS Trusts and Primary Care Trusts greater freedom to provide social care and would allow social services in-house providers to provide some community health services on behalf of the NHS.

These powers will be permissive, which means that it will be up to local and health authorities to decide between themselves which arrangements if any will be most helpful for their joint working. What works locally is what counts.

The new NHS

6.11 More widely, local authorities will be crucial partners in the new
approaches to health and health care set out in the White Paper
The new NHS and the Green Paper *Our Healthier Nation*. This will
involve local authorities in their wider corporate role, covering for
example, public health responsibilities, community safety, and
housing and regeneration plans. But social services will obviously be
the main local authority responsibility which will contribute to and
benefit from these new arrangements.

'local authorities will be crucial partners in the new NHS'

'social services will be involved in the governance arrangements for Primary Care Groups and Primary Care Trusts'

6.12 At national level, as described in Chapter 7, we have introduced National Priorities Guidance covering both the NHS and social services. At local level, Health Improvement Programmes, to be introduced from April 1999, will bring together a range of health and local government services to work with others towards common objectives to improve the health and well-being of local communities. Social services will need to take account of that strategic framework in planning their own services. At operational level, they will need to draw up with the NHS Joint Investment Plans based on commonly agreed objectives for vulnerable groups. Social services will also be involved in the governance arrangements for Primary Care Groups and Primary Care Trusts being set up from April 1999, for which shadow arrangements are already being established now.

The new NHS – partnership with social services

The White Paper *The new NHS* set out the Government's plans to modernise the NHS by replacing the internal market with a system of integrated care based on partnership and driven by performance. The White Paper described further new initiatives to continue the drive for improved working at the NHS and local government interface. These initiatives included:

- a **new statutory duty of partnership** on all local bodies in the NHS family and on local authorities to work together to promote the well-being of their local communities – this gives substance to the co-operation necessary to bring about improvements in health and social care

- provision for **local authority Chief Executives to participate in health authority meetings**

- establishment of **Primary Care Groups** to improve the health of their local population, develop primary care and community health services, and commission hospital services – these groups will work closely with social services on both planning and delivery of services; and will have social services representation on their governing bodies

- the introduction of **Health Improvement Programmes** for each health authority area to provide the local strategy for improving health and health care with involvement from partner agencies such as local government and voluntary bodies

- a key element of the Health Improvement Programme in each area will be **Joint Investment Plans**, drawn up between health and social services to deal particularly with groups where coordinated services are most important.

6.13 This presents a demanding and exciting agenda, which should mean that social services can do more for the people they try to help. It will require a new way of thinking, which in turn will require the investment of management and staff time both in local authority social services and in partner agencies. The Department of Health will provide support through the dissemination of good practice and local development work through the Social Care and NHS Regional Offices.

Partnerships in services for drug misusers

6.14 Drug misuse is an important area where social services work not only with the NHS, but with many other local interests, such as housing, the probation service and the police. The Government's Drugs Strategy White Paper, *Tackling Drugs to Build a Better Britain,* sets out a ten year plan for addressing the problems of drug misuse and identifies a central role for social services in delivering the strategy's objectives. The White Paper recommends that "funding for the purchase of community care services for drug misusers should be given adequate priority by local authorities. The Department of Health should take steps to ensure that this money is used for drugs-specific partnership work, with mechanisms put in place to ensure that current expenditure on drug misusers from community care funding is protected."

6.15 The Government has committed itself to the new strategy, and following the Comprehensive Spending Review has allocated £20.5 million of new money over three years to enable the commissioning of additional community care services for drug misusers in support of locally agreed Drug Action Team plans.

Partnership with housing

6.16 Housing is an essential element in the network of community care services. The Audit Commission estimate that around £2 billion a year is spent on housing-related community care services for around 1.3 million people. There are some 450,000 placements by local authorities and housing associations in sheltered housing with wardens on site – similar to the total number of residential and nursing home places. Yet, a recent Audit Commission report found that collaboration between housing and social services is still often

"A picture emerges of inadequate identification of needs, inflexible use of stock and insufficient early intervention to prevent vulnerable people reaching crisis point."

"None of the fieldwork authorities conveyed a clear vision of the future role of sheltered housing. There is little evidence of joint working with social services and local Registered Social Landlords to include sheltered housing in a wider strategic approach to services for older people…".

"In effect, many people with mental health problems become trapped in the "revolving door" syndrome whereby tenancy crisis leads to hospitalisation and/or homelessness, and then a lack of on-going support after being rehoused means that these tenants fail to establish a firm foothold in the community."

Home Alone, Audit Commission, 1997

'*the Government recognises the crucial role housing has to play in community care*'

weak, and the full potential of housing departments and providers to contribute to community care is not being exploited.

6.17 The Government recognises the crucial role housing has to play in community care and the need for partnership between health, housing and social services in supporting people in the community. This partnership needs to involve not only the statutory authorities but also housing providers to ensure that housing needs are identified and strategies developed to address them. In areas with two-tier local government, social services are the responsibility of the county council while housing is the responsibility of the district councils, so there is an additional boundary to overcome in these cases.

6.18 The Department of Health and the Department of the Environment, Transport and the Regions have worked together to assist them with this. We have produced joint guidance to assist health, housing and social services to develop strategic plans and, more recently, the *Making Partnerships Work in Community Care* workbook to help frontline workers to make the connections locally. This is being backed up by joint work between the Social Care Regions and the Government Offices for the Regions to promote the messages in the workbook to local housing, social services, and health professionals working at the interface between housing and care and support services.

6.19 Examples of further work at national level are:

- the current inter-departmental review to establish a modern, practicable and sustainable arrangement for the long-term funding of supported accommodation

- changes to the building regulations to make all new homes more accessible to disabled people

- a commitment to give local authorities new powers to provide community alarms to a wider range of people.

6.20 At a local level we are:

- working closely with the National Housing Federation to improve service standards in housing and support schemes through its "Framework for Housing with Support"

- preparing guidance for local authorities on housing options for people with a mental illness or learning disability.

6.21 But the Audit Commission report makes it clear that there is more to be done. The joint DETR/DH guidance provides a firm foundation for authorities to address the Audit Commission criticisms. Development of the Long-term Care Charter, with its emphasis on housing as well as health and social services, will build on this and give increasing clarity about what users can expect and how authorities should jointly assess their respective performance.

6.22 As described in Chapter 3, the Government is taking steps to help young people leaving the care of local authorities, who often face great difficulty in finding suitable and affordable accommodation. It is essential that the relevant agencies – social services, housing authorities, other housing providers, and voluntary agencies – come together to assess and plan to meet the accommodation needs of care leavers, as well as other vulnerable young people. The Government will issue guidance to social services to accompany the forthcoming revised Housing Allocation and Homelessness Code of Guidance from the DETR. This will make it clear that when placed in mainstream or social housing, young people formerly looked after may need a great deal of personal and other support to sustain them in the community and help them meet their responsibilities as tenants. They must also receive assistance and support to develop life skills so that they can live independently in the future.

6.23 More widely, social services can make an important contribution to wider local authority-led programmes to tackle the problems of homelessness, poor housing conditions, and social exclusion in deprived neighbourhoods. These issues, and the need for co-ordinated local approaches to tackle them, have been covered in the Social Exclusion Unit's reports on rough sleepers and on neighbourhood renewal.

Better housing for disabled people

On 9 March 1998 the Government announced that Part M of the Building Regulations, covering access and facilities for disabled people, is to be extended to include new dwellings. The purpose of these proposed measures is to allow people to be able to remain in their own homes longer as they get older, and to make it easier for disabled people to visit the homes of friends or relatives.

In practice this means that in future, new homes will generally include a level or gently sloping approach, a wide entrance without steps, adequate circulation, wider internal doors and a toilet on the ground floor to enable access by wheelchair users. This will result in more homes that are accessible to disabled people.

Social Exclusion Unit reports

Rough sleeping

The report *Rough Sleeping* describes the factors that contribute to people sleeping rough, and identifies the gaps in services available to them. Only five per cent of rough sleepers do so by choice. There are not enough beds, not enough help with drug, alcohol or mental illness problems, and a job and a home can prove impossible to secure. Many cannot register with a GP and health outcomes are very poor, with the mortality rate 25 times higher than the national average.

The report sets in train a strategy, to cut the number of people sleeping rough by two thirds by 2002. This includes a major programme to prevent rough sleeping by ensuring that people leaving institutions are better equipped to live on their own and are not left to fend for themselves. A new body will be established to bring effective co-ordination and direction to services for rough sleepers in London, and outside London the Department of the Environment, Transport and the Regions and the Department of Health will co-ordinate help for rough sleepers.

Neighbourhood renewal

The report *Bringing Britain Together: A Strategy for Neighbourhood Renewal* describes the effects of poverty, unemployment, poor health, crime and lack of access to services in deprived neighbourhoods. It also identifies the success stories from around the country where communities have come together to find solutions to their own local problems.

The report sets in train a national strategy to support neighbourhood renewal. Eighteen Policy Action Teams, drawn from 10 Government Departments and involving experts from outside government, will focus on a range of issues including getting people into work, improving the management and fabric of neighbourhoods, building a future for young people, improving access to services and getting Government to work better for local communities.

The New Deal for Communities will support this work by providing £800 million funding over the next three years for the intensive regeneration of neighbourhoods.

Partnership with the employment service

6.24 As mentioned in Chapter 2, social services also have a part to play in achieving our aim of work for those who can. They have a key role in working with disabled people, in partnership with other agencies, to ensure appropriate, timely, cost effective and consistent support. Such partnerships and joint working benefit the individual through helping them to an independent life in the community; and the employer through enabling them to recruit employees that are motivated. Effective social services will help disabled people to get and stay in work where they need help, for example before leaving for work; and will work closely with local employment services at an early stage to provide integrated support for someone facing the onset of a disability so as to maintain maximum independence. Social services will need to work closely with the Single Gateway we have proposed to enable it to act as a single point of access to welfare.

Education and other children's services

6.25 In children's social services, partnership with the education service are at least as important as those with the health service. Since both social services and education are the responsibility of the same authorities in every part of the country, there are no organisational excuses for poor co-ordination. However, joint working is frequently poor, and in general, children's social services often suffer a high degree of isolation from the rest of the local authority.

6.26 Chapter 3 makes clear that the welfare of children must be seen as a corporate responsibility of the entire local authority, and social services for children must be seen as an element of that wider responsibility. Some authorities are tackling this through using their management arrangements to bring together a range of services affecting children. Whatever the management arrangements in place, every authority must bring the resources of all its departments to bear to improve children's social services. The objectives for children's social services identified in Chapter 3 require inter-agency co-operation and will, in turn, deliver benefits to other services. And the Quality Protects initiative, also mentioned in Chapter 3, is directed at each local authority as a whole, not just at social services functions for children.

'the welfare of children must be seen as a corporate responsibility of the entire local authority'

6.27 We will reinforce this council-wide responsibility by redefining the requirements for children's services planning. We will place the duty to plan on the local authority as a whole, and require them to include specific proposals, for example, to:

- improve the health and education of looked after children

- determine priorities for improving support for children in need, including disabled children and those with emotional and behavioural difficulties, and set out how those priorities will be given effect

- address housing needs of families with children in need

- summarise the outcomes intended in youth justice, behaviour support, and early years plans, and thus bring together action on behalf of the main groups of children at risk of social exclusion.

6.28 These children's services plans will need to be agreed with all interested agencies, and arrangements established to monitor the outcomes. Social services will need to work with interested parties to ensure they recognise that effective expenditure and action in these areas could reduce the resources needed in other areas and in the future; to obtain the necessary commitment and ownership from them to ensure that agreed plans can be achieved; and to ensure that outcomes are effectively monitored.

6.29 This change to the status of children's services plans will need legislation which we intend to introduce when Parliamentary time allows. Current guidance encourages, but cannot require, authorities to cover all services for children and families. In addition, although legislation requires social services to consult with other departments and organisations there is no requirement that those consulted respond or participate in planning. In future all interested parties will be required by statute to participate in and take responsibility for their role in children's services planning. In the meantime, we will rely on inter-departmentally issued guidance.

Criminal justice agencies – youth justice

6.30 The Government has undertaken a comprehensive review of youth justice issues. New structures for work with young offenders are to be set up under the Crime and Disorder Act. Multi-agency youth offending teams are to be established by local authorities with social services and education responsibilities, in partnership with health authorities, the police and the probation service. A draft inter-departmental circular *Establishing Youth Offending Teams* explained the important role that social services and health authorities will have within these teams. This is linked with their broader work on the welfare and health of young offenders and children and young people at risk of offending. Pilots of the teams began on 30 September 1998 in selected areas and will run for a total of eighteen months, with a view to implementing them nationally by April 2000. A new national body – the Youth Justice Board for England and Wales – has been established to advise Ministers on setting standards for service delivery and to monitor performance across the youth justice system, including youth offending teams.

Other partnerships

6.31 As well as these partnerships between social services and other public agencies, there are important partnerships with the voluntary sector, with independent social care providers, and indeed with users, carers, and their representatives. A partnership approach should underlie the relationships that social services have with all these groups.

Partnership with the voluntary sector

Voluntary organisations make an enormous contribution to social care, working alongside and in co-operation with social services. Social services should have good relationships with voluntary organisations, both in service provision partnerships and also in order to help understand the needs and views of users. Local authorities should ensure that they know which voluntary organisations are in their area; what the voluntary sector can contribute to meeting the needs of the local population; and where the authority's support for the sector can be used to best effect. In November 1998 the Home Office and a voluntary sector representative group jointly launched a *Compact on Relations between Government and the Voluntary and Community Sector in England*, setting out agreed principles for effective working relationships. Authorities are encouraged to adopt these principles and to establish their own versions of the Compact.

7

Key themes

- *new systems for monitoring how well services are delivered*
- *clear objectives and priorities*
- *central and local government working together to ensure high standards*

Improving delivery and efficiency

making sure it happens

Introduction

'the delivery of social care to the people of this country is a substantial task, costing £9 billion'

7.1 The delivery of social care to the people of this country is a substantial task, costing £9 billion. It involves dealing with a huge variety of people in need in practically every part of the country, from rural villages to densely-populated inner city areas. Managing such an operation is a complex and demanding job. High quality and good value services can only be achieved if there are sound management, information and performance systems in place. Checks are needed both locally and nationally to make sure that people are getting the modern and dependable social services that they deserve.

7.2 The SSI/Audit Commission Joint Reviews are providing invaluable information on how social services are being delivered throughout the country, in terms of quality of services, effectiveness of delivery, and value for money. It is the first time that such a comprehensive picture of social services performance has been available, and it is instructive. With the number of reviews completed now more than 30, the Joint Reviews have found many examples of good practice, including some authorities who are delivering good quality social services across the board. However, they have also found too many examples of poor services, widespread inefficiency, and a worryingly high number of authorities with serious and deep-rooted problems.

7.3 This situation must change. Improvements are needed in the quality and value for money of social services and to ensure that local people are receiving the services that, as taxpayers, they should expect. There is much that local authorities can do to improve their services, and to drive up their standards to match those of the best. But local authorities cannot deliver all the necessary improvements on their own. The Government accepts that it has responsibilities for ensuring the effective delivery of social services, and will work in partnership with local authorities to achieve continuous improvement.

'drive up standards to match those of the best'

Getting the framework right

7.4 Whilst social services are locally-managed services meeting local needs they operate within the framework of legislation and policy set by Government. In the past Government has not done all that it could to support the local delivery of social services or to assist local authorities in improving their performance. The proposals in this White Paper address this, and enable the Government to promote better management of social services. At a national level the Government will provide the proper context for social services by:

- establishing clear objectives for social services, creating a clear expectation of the outcomes social services are required to deliver

- publishing National Priorities Guidance, setting out the key targets for social services to achieve in the medium term

- providing the resources to support the achievement of demonstrable change

- putting in place effective systems to monitor and manage performance.

Clear objectives

> *'social services need direction if they are to serve people better'*

7.5 Social services need direction if they are to serve people better. The new national objectives for social services arising from the Comprehensive Spending Review and set out below provide this direction. The action set out for adult and children's services in Chapters 2 and 3 of this White Paper address the areas where improvement is most needed. This is the first time that any Government has laid out explicitly its expectations of social services. This clarity will allow local authorities to focus their efforts, and provide them with the guidance they need to carry through the programme of change necessary to modernise social services. The monitoring arrangements described in this Chapter will allow progress against the national objectives as a whole, and of the action identified for adult and children's services, to be assessed both locally and nationally.

National priorities guidance

7.6 The agenda embodied in the new objectives for social services is a challenging and significant one. Over time we wish to see improvements in performance against each of the objectives. But we recognise that this will take time and that there is a need to prioritise. *Modernising Health and Social Services*, the National Priorities Guidance (NPG) sets out the key priorities for 1999/00 – 2001/02 at national level for both health and social services:

National priorities for health and social care 1999/2000 – 2001/02

Social services lead	Shared lead	NHS lead
• Children's welfare	• Cutting health inequalities	• Waiting lists/times
• Inter-agency working	• Mental health	• Primary care
• Regulation	• Promoting independence	• Coronary heart disease
		• Cancer

National objectives for social services

Children's services

- to ensure that children are securely attached to carers capable of providing safe and effective care for the duration of childhood

- to ensure that children are protected from emotional, physical, sexual abuse and neglect (significant harm)

- to ensure that children in need gain maximum life chance benefits from educational opportunities, health care and social care

- to ensure that children looked after gain maximum life chance benefits from educational opportunities, health care and social care

- to ensure that young people leaving care, as they enter adulthood, are not isolated and participate socially and economically as citizens

- to ensure that children with specific social needs arising out of disability or a health condition are living in families or other appropriate settings in the community where their assessed needs are adequately met and reviewed

- to ensure that referral and assessment processes discriminate effectively between different types and levels of need and produce a timely service response.

Adult services

- to promote the independence of adults assessed as needing social care support arranged by the local authority, respecting their dignity and furthering their social and economic participation

- to enable adults assessed as needing social care support to live as safe, full and as normal a life as possible, in their own home wherever feasible

- to ensure that people of working age who have been assessed as requiring community care services, are provided with these services in ways which take account of and, as far as possible, maximise their and their carers' capacity to take up, remain in or return to employment

- to work with the NHS, users, carers and other agencies to avoid unnecessary admission to hospital, and inappropriate placement on leaving hospital; and to maximise the health status and thus independence of those they support

- to enable informal carers to care or continue to care for as long as they and the service user wish

- to plan, commission, purchase and monitor an adequate supply of appropriate, cost-effective and safe social care provision for those eligible for local authority support

- to identify individuals with social care needs who are eligible for public support, to assess those needs accurately and consistently, and to review care packages as necessary to ensure that they continue to be appropriate and effective.

Common objectives

- to actively involve users and carers in planning services and in tailoring individual packages of care; and to ensure effective mechanisms are in place to handle complaints

- to ensure through regulatory powers and duties that adults and children in regulated services are protected from harm and poor care standards

- to ensure that social care workers are appropriately skilled, trained and qualified, and to promote the uptake of training at all levels

- to maximise the benefit to service users for the resources available, and to demonstrate the effectiveness and value for money of the care and support provided, and allow for choice and different responses for different needs and circumstances. For adult services, to operate a charging regime which is transparent, consistent and equitable; and which maximises revenue while not providing distortions or disincentives which would affect the outcomes of care for individuals.

7.7 These national priorities have been drawn from the whole of the Government's modernisation programme, both the vision for social care articulated in this White Paper and that for the NHS and public health as set out in *The new NHS* and *Our Healthier Nation.* Delivering the objectives set in each of the priority areas will be an important first step in the Government's programme to modernise health and social care.

7.8 Although the NHS has had similar guidance in the past, this is a new departure for social services and reflects the Government's determination to provide a clear lead to social services. The fact that it is joint guidance makes clear the extent to which health and social services are interdependent. *Modernising Health and Social Services* was published on 30 September 1998.

The resources to deliver change

'*this is investment for reform and the Government expects to see improvements in quality and efficiency in return for the increased investment*'

7.9 The Government is providing new resources to support the programme of modernisation. This is investment for reform and the Government expects to see improvements in quality and efficiency in return for the increased funding.

7.10 In the White Paper *Modern Public Services: Investing in Reform,* the Government set out firm three-year plans for each major spending programme. The total funding for social services will be increased by an annual average of 3.1 per cent above inflation over the next three years – a clear signal of the priority the Government is giving to this area of spending. Knowledge of the Government's future financial intentions should help authorities to plan the delivery of services with greater confidence and enable them to look beyond a single year horizon.

7.11 To support the delivery of reform we are introducing a new Social Services Modernisation Fund which will target grant funding on priority areas. Whilst the Modernisation Fund will provide significant resources, success in modernising social services will be dependent on the effective use of all resources, and the Modernisation Fund will be used as a lever for delivering reform across all social services activity and expenditure.

7.12 The Modernisation Fund will deliver over £1.3 billion of additional resources over the three years 1999/2000 – 2001/2002. Taking this together with the increase in funding delivered through Standard Spending Assessments (SSAs), and the increases in the existing grants for specialist services such as HIV/AIDS and drug and alcohol services, there will be in total nearly £3 billion extra resources for social services over the next three years.

Delivering improved performance

7.13 The Government's White Paper, *Modern Local Government: In Touch with the People*, sets out the Government's proposals for Best Value, a rigorous and systematic approach to improving local authority performance. This will enable authorities to demonstrate to their electorate and to central government that they are achieving best value in carrying out their responsibilities. The Best Value regime will apply to all local government functions, including social services.

7.14 Best Value will be a duty to deliver services to clear standards – covering both quality and cost – by the most effective, economic and efficient means available. The aim of the Best Value process is to secure continuous improvements in performance, and to deliver services which bear comparison to the best. Local authorities will be accountable to local people and have a responsibility to central government in its role as representative of the broader national interest.

7.15 Local authorities will set targets for improvements in both quality and efficiency of these services. Meeting those targets will allow them to demonstrate best value. Government will provide a clear lead in relation to performance standards and targets where it judges the national interest requires it. For social services Government will set targets for both quality, as set out in the National Priorities Guidance, and efficiency.

'local authorities will be accountable to local people and have a responsibility to central government'

The Best Value performance management framework

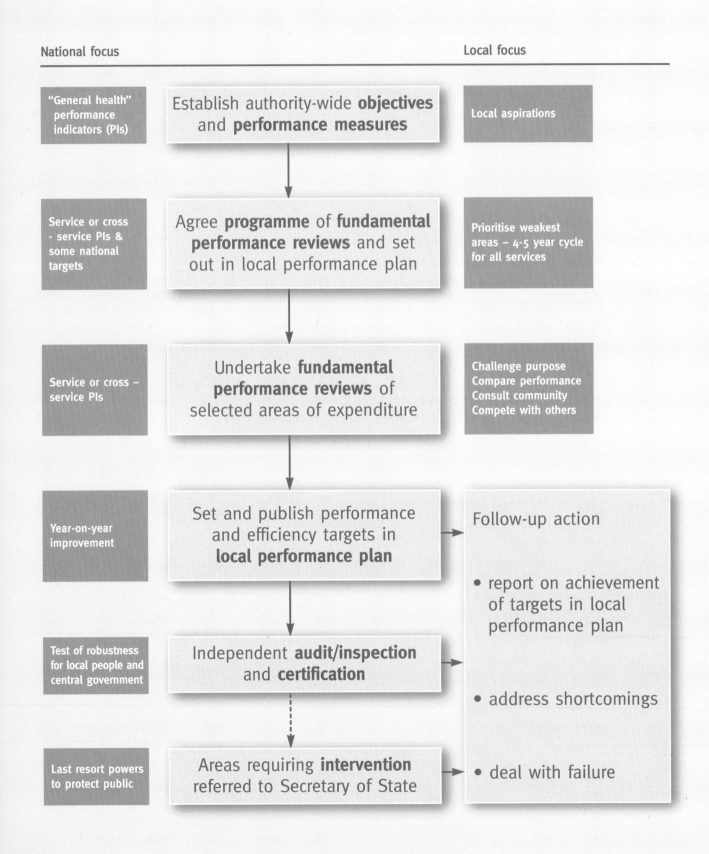

National focus

Local focus

"General health" performance indicators (PIs)	Establish authority-wide **objectives** and **performance measures**	Local aspirations
Service or cross - service PIs & some national targets	Agree **programme** of **fundamental performance reviews** and set out in local performance plan	Prioritise weakest areas – 4-5 year cycle for all services
Service or cross – service PIs	Undertake **fundamental performance reviews** of selected areas of expenditure	Challenge purpose Compare performance Consult community Compete with others
Year-on-year improvement	Set and publish performance and efficiency targets in **local performance plan**	Follow-up action

• report on achievement of targets in local performance plan |
| Test of robustness for local people and central government | Independent **audit/inspection** and **certification** | • address shortcomings |
| Last resort powers to protect public | Areas requiring **intervention** referred to Secretary of State | • deal with failure |

7.16 Analysis by the Department of Health and others, including the Personal Social Services Research Unit at the University of Kent, has shown falling efficiency in social services over several years. In simple terms, this means that for every extra £1 of funding, less than £1's worth of service has resulted. The findings of the Joint Reviews confirm this and suggest that there is considerable scope for social services authorities to make savings by improving efficiency. The reviews have found evidence of four and fivefold variations between authorities in the costs of providing the same service. The Government has therefore decided to set targets for improvements in the efficiency with which social services are delivered. In 1999/00, the target will be a 2 per cent improvement in efficiency. In 2000/01, by which time it is expected that the duty of Best Value will apply, a further 2 per cent improvement will be required, followed by a further 3 per cent improvement in 2001/02. The Government will closely monitor progress against these targets.

'evidence of four and fivefold variations between authorities in the costs of providing the same service'

7.17 Best Value will introduce new performance management arrangements into local government to ensure that best value is achieved. The Department of Health is reorganising its approach to performance management so that it is aligned with and builds upon the local Best Value arrangements. The main elements of local and national performance management activity to be introduced for social services are outlined below:

- local authorities will establish **authority wide objectives** and performance measures. Local objectives for social services will need to reflect the national objectives and the need to meet any Government-prescribed national standards or targets, such as those in the National Priorities Guidance (NPG)

- local authorities will carry out **fundamental performance reviews** of all their services over a five year cycle; the outcomes of these service specific reviews will inform the preparation of local performance plans, and be assessed as part of Joint Reviews

- the local planning process will be supported by information from a new statistical **performance assessment framework**. This will draw together the key statistical information on the performance of social services. The Best Value National Performance Indicators will be central in this framework, supplemented by a number of further performance indicators to give a more rounded and in-depth

'common understanding between central and local government on performance'

assessment of performance. The performance assessment framework will provide a basis for a common understanding between central and local government on performance, value for money and resourcing issues in social services, both at overall programme level and in terms of individual local authorities. The performance indicators from the framework will allow authorities to compare their performance on a consistent basis. A similar framework is being developed for the NHS. Taken together, the two frameworks will enable the performance of local and health authorities at this vital interface to be examined, and key issues identified for action. It will be important for social services to have sound and effective information systems in place, in order to have a good understanding of how well they are performing against national indicators and against their own indicators

- **local performance plans** will provide a clear practical expression of an authority's performance. The plans will identify targets for annual improvements against locally defined performance indicators and the National Best Value Performance Indicators reflecting the quality and effectiveness of social services. In those areas where it is judged necessary the Government will also set performance standards which all authorities will be expected to meet

- the Department of Health through the Social Care Regional Offices, with appropriate contributions from the NHS Regional Offices, will carry out **annual reviews** of the social services aspects **of the local performance plan**. These reviews will also provide an opportunity to discuss the delivery of specific policy initiatives, to assess with the NHS Executive local joint working with the NHS, and to pick up any issues from recent SSI inspections and Joint Reviews. We will strengthen the Social Care Regional Offices to enable them to take a more active role in monitoring and reviewing social services performance

- **independent inspection** by the SSI both of individual authorities and on thematic issues across sample authorities will continue, the overall programme being discussed annually with the Local Government Association and the Association of Directors of Social Services. Methodologies for these inspections will increasingly be informed and underpinned by the data in the performance assessment framework

- **Joint Reviews** of every authority: the resourcing of the Joint Review programme will be expanded to enable each of the 150 local authorities to be reviewed every five years, rather than every seven years as at present, consistent with the five year cycle of the Best Value regime.

Social services performance assessment framework

The areas of performance to be covered by the performance assessment framework are shown in the table alongside the definitions for the areas and some example performance indicators. We will consult shortly on the details of the performance assessment framework.

Area of performance: national priorities and strategic objectives

Definition	Examples of possible performance indicators
• the extent to which local social services authorities (LSSAs) are delivering the national priorities for social care (as set out in the NPG), the national objectives and their own local strategic objectives	• the proportion of children looked after who have 3 or more placements in one year • emergency admissions to hospital of people aged over 75

Area of performance: cost and efficiency

• the extent to which LSSAs provide cost effective and efficient services	• unit costs, composite measures for adult and children's services

Area of performance: effectiveness of service delivery and outcomes

• the extent to which services are appropriate to need; in line with best practice; to agreed standards; timely; and delivered by appropriately trained staff and • LSSA success in using its resources to increase self sufficiency and social and economic participation; to increase life chances of looked after children; to provide safe and supportive services	• emergency psychiatric readmissions • the proportion of children who were looked after at age 16 still in touch with social services at age 19 • the number of households receiving intensive home care per 1,000 households headed by someone aged 75 or over, adjusted by SSA • the percentage of inspections of residential homes for adults which should have been carried out that were carried out

Area of performance: quality of services for users and carers

• user/carer perceptions and experiences of services; responsiveness of services to individual needs; continuity of provision; involvement of users/carers in assessment and review	• delayed discharge from hospital • proportion of residents provided with single rooms • user and carer satisfaction surveys

Area of performance: fair access

• the fairness of provision in relation to need, the existence of clear eligibility criteria, the provision of accessible information about the provision of services	• people aged 65+ helped to live at home • daycare provision for adults per head of population, adjusted by SSA • children looked after per 1,000 population, adjusted by SSA

'the Government will consider means of rewarding local authorities that are delivering effective social services, and will not hesitate to intervene where services are failing'

7.18 The framework set out above will provide local authorities with the evidence and tools they need to improve performance. The Government will consider means of rewarding local authorities that are delivering effective social services, and will not hesitate to intervene where services are failing.

Beacon services

7.19 Good practice should be recognised and rewarded. Social services are rightly criticised for their failings, but we hear too little praise for their successes. The new performance framework will help identify and publicise good performance, through the publication of authorities' performance against the indicators in the performance assessment framework and through the work of the SSI and Joint Reviews. The Social Care Regional Offices will be able to facilitate the exchange of good practice and the pairing of authorities who could learn from each other.

7.20 The best authorities will be able to apply for beacon status. Beacon councils will be recognised centres of expertise and excellence that everyone should look to. The Government will consult widely on the details of the beacon councils including the rewards associated with beacon status and how the scheme will apply to social services.

Interventions

7.21 The Government will work to help authorities to tackle poor performance, and will act in partnership with the Local Government Association where appropriate. Where there are serious failures, the Government will be prepared to take firm action to secure improvement, including using statutory powers to intervene when necessary. The Government will act to protect vulnerable people who are put at risk by poor services, and it will ensure that it has the statutory powers at its disposal to do this. The White Paper *Modern Local Government: In Touch with the People* sets out the range of interventions the Government intends to put in place through legislation to underpin Best Value. They include requiring:

- an authority to draw up an action plan for improvement, and deliver a specified level of performance by a set date

- an authority to accept external management help

- responsibility to be transferred to another authority or third party in case of serious service failure.

7.22 These powers will be available to the Secretary of State for Health to enable him to intervene where local social services authorities are failing to deliver best value.

Public and private sector provision

7.23 Best value must be secured in all social services, whether provided in-house or contracted out to the voluntary or private sector. This Government does not take an ideological approach to this issue, and has no preconception about whether the public or the voluntary or private sector should be the preferred providers. These decisions should be based entirely on judgements about best value and optimum outcomes for individual users, and authorities must be able to demonstrate that their arrangements are delivering this.

7.24 By the same token, we are keen to remove any distorting effects there are in the current system for authorities to use one sector over the other, and keen to give councils as much flexibility as possible in making effective use of public money available for care. One example of this is the Residential Allowance. This allowance is a component of Income Support, and is payable to residents placed in voluntary or private residential care or nursing homes. It is not available to people placed in local authorities' own homes. The individual does not see the money, as it goes direct to payment of the placement. It provides a subsidy towards the costs to social services of providing this type of residential accommodation, thereby reducing their contribution to such placements. However, it can also act as a perverse incentive to place people in residential care because it would be less costly to social services than keeping them at home.

'Best value must be secured in all social services, whether in-house or contracted out'

7.25 We believe there is a strong case for phasing out the payment of the Residential Allowance, and for transferring resources, via a special grant, to local authorities. This would not be a loss to the individuals concerned, and in effect it would simply move funding from one part of the system to another. But it would create a level playing field between public, private and voluntary sector provision. In particular, it would support the agenda set out in this White Paper by giving authorities more flexibility to use the resources in promoting independence. This could include, for instance, better services to people at home, possibly through greater use of direct payments.

7.26 The Government would need to work through the implication of this change on overall costs. We would want, for example, to consider the implications for other areas of public expenditure and ensure that the change would not lead to a greater use of local authorities' own residential care homes where these cost more without a gain in quality of care. We will also need to assess the impact of any change on the take-up of other DSS benefits, and on independent sector care homes (although reduced use of residential care would provide new opportunities for independent domiciliary care providers). We will therefore consider the detailed options carefully and consult with both local authorities and voluntary and private sector interests before deciding whether and how to implement any change.

Member responsibilities and scrutiny

7.27 To go with the new national framework described above, local authorities have a corporate responsibility for ensuring that best value social services are being delivered to their citizens. It is important that this responsibility is given due importance by elected members in particular. Authorities will be in a position to improve delivery and efficiency by:

- having clear responsibilities for social services at member level, including arrangements for the review of policy and strong scrutiny arrangements for social services performance; and

- having management and accountability structures that provide the most effective services.

7.28 It has been stressed elsewhere in this White Paper that where the welfare of children is at stake – and most particularly when the local authority is acting as corporate parent for children looked after – it is essential that elected members ensure that services are up to standard. This is true for all social services, and authorities will need to establish proper scrutiny arrangements to check how well they are performing.

7.29 Scrutiny is required at two levels. Firstly, those elected members who are responsible for social services (in future these may be the designated executive cabinet members rather than committee chairs) must ensure that they have the capacity to monitor and scrutinise the performance of the Director of Social Services and his/her staff – it is not generally acceptable for elected members to claim that they are shocked when evidence emerges of serious service failures. Such failures should not go unnoticed.

7.30 Secondly, under the new arrangements for political decision-making in local government, there will be scrutiny arrangements for "backbench" councillors to hold the executive to account. They will examine, in public, members of the executive and senior officers on the services being provided and the policies being pursued and proposed. They will also consider strategic issues and the overall performance of local social services. Authorities should ensure that they provide for full scrutiny of social services functions, perhaps through a specific scrutiny committee for social services.

Management structures

7.31 As a result of the changes to local government structures, the Local Authority Social Services Act 1970 will need significant amendment. In particular, there will in future be no requirement for a Social Services Committee, given that committees will no longer be the model for decision-making in local government. However, as stressed above, member responsibilities for social services will remain crucial under the new arrangements.

7.32 The Government will retain the legal requirement for every social services authority to appoint a Director of Social Services, who

Mayors and cabinets: new structures in local government

The White Paper *Modern Local Government: In Touch with the People* set out the Government's programme to modernise local government, including significant changes to the committee-based system which has existed in local government for over a century. Authorities will be required to draw up proposals for new structures based on a clear distinction between executive responsibilities and the other roles of elected members. Instead of decision by committee, in future there will be streamlined and more accountable structures, with arrangements such as executive cabinets and executive mayors.

These changes will be positive for social services. The new structures are intended to provide stronger and clearer accountability to locally elected members, and the proposed new scrutiny arrangements will give "backbench" councillors a better opportunity to hold the executive to account on social services performance.

'member responsibilities for social services will remain crucial under the new arrangements'

'legal requirement for every social services authority to appoint a Director of Social Services'

must be directly accountable to the Chief Executive and must have direct access to elected members on social services matters. The Government has no wish to impose detailed management structures for authorities' social services – most authorities operate a "traditional" social services department, but an increasing number of authorities have adopted alternative and innovative arrangements. However authorities choose to structure their management, they must be in a position to show that they can meet all their statutory requirements and that their arrangements provide safe and effective social services.

7.33 In particular all authorities will need to identify:

- named councillor(s) who will carry the executive responsibility for the whole range of social services responsibilities

- how the elected member scrutiny arrangements will monitor the performance of the council's social services responsibilities

- clear accountability arrangements for all social services responsibilities to the Director of Social Services

- where social services functions are discharged across a number of separate internal management structures or council departments, clearly defined liaison and accountability arrangements (for example, those responsible for mental health services must ensure that they consider child welfare issues where a parent has a mental illness, and work with the child protection team wherever necessary)

- adequate arrangements for managing information relating to the social services functions as a whole (for example, dissemination of guidance, collection of financial and statistical data, liaison with the SSI and Joint Reviews).

7.34 While allowing authorities the freedom to manage their social services as they think best, the Government intends to monitor these arrangements as part of the performance management arrangements described earlier in this Chapter. In keeping with this approach, the Government will also remove the current requirement for Directors of Social Services to seek permission from the Secretary of State before taking on non-social services functions (Section 6(5) of the Local Authority Social Services Act 1970).

Conclusion

7.35 The proposals in this Chapter respond to the need for new political structures as part of the modernisation of local government and will remove existing impediments to this process. They also recognise the need for a greater emphasis on raising standards of performance in social services. The introduction of Best Value will provide social services authorities with a framework within which to assess their performance, establish standards and set targets for improvement. The Government will work alongside authorities to ensure that real improvements are delivered.

'the proposals in this Chapter respond to the need for new political structures as part of the modernisation of local government'

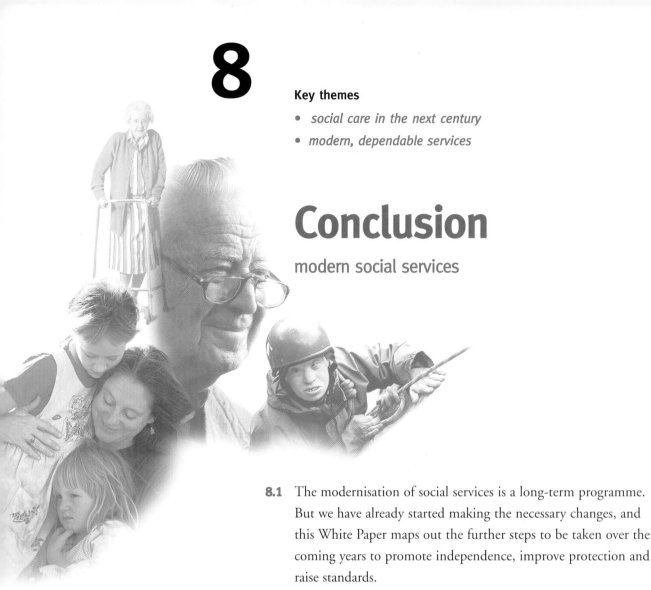

8

Key themes
- *social care in the next century*
- *modern, dependable services*

Conclusion

modern social services

8.1 The modernisation of social services is a long-term programme. But we have already started making the necessary changes, and this White Paper maps out the further steps to be taken over the coming years to promote independence, improve protection and raise standards.

8.2 If we achieve the goals that we have set for improvement in social services, in the early years of the next century the people of this country will experience a modern and dependable service that matches the aspirations set out in the introductory chapter to this White Paper:

- services will promote and enhance people's independence, with better prevention and rehabilitation services established with the help of the additional funding the Government is providing; and many more people will use direct payments schemes to have real control over how their care needs are provided for

- services will meet each individual's needs, with social services providing an integrated service with the NHS and other agencies, pooling budgets where appropriate

- care services will be organised, accessed, provided and financed in a fair, open and consistent way in every part of the country. National Service Frameworks will ensure that the services needed are available everywhere, and the Fair Access to Care initiative will bring fairness and transparency into the decisions on whether people qualify for support

'services will promote and enhance people's independence, with better prevention and rehabilitation services'

- children looked after by local authorities will benefit from the radical improvements to be made to the care system, backed up by substantial extra funding. Better arrangements for their education and health care will be in place, and they can be assured of a better deal when they come to leave care and start their adult life

- everyone will be safeguarded against abuse, neglect or poor treatment while receiving care. Standards will be clearer, checks will be tighter and the regional Commissions for Care Standards will have strong and swift powers to put a stop to any abuse where it occurs

- social care staff will have clearer standards and better training arrangements, overseen by the General Social Care Council. This will benefit both the staff and the people receiving care, who can feel assured that the staff they deal with are safe, skilled and competent

- and people will be able to have confidence in their local social services, knowing that through the Best Value regime, checks are made both locally and nationally to ensure that services are up to scratch, and action can be taken where standards are not met.

8.3 A service that demonstrates all these features will be one in which public confidence can be restored, and one on which we can all rely.

'a service that demonstrates all these features will be one in which public confidence can be restored, and one on which we can all rely'

Bibliography

Audit Commission for Local Authorities and the National Health
Service in England and Wales
Home alone: the role of housing in community care
London: Audit Commission, 1998

Burgner T, Department of Health, Welsh Office
The regulation and inspection of social services
London: Department of Health, 1996

Cabinet Office Social Exclusion Unit
Rough sleeping
London: The Stationery Office, 1998. (Cm. 4008)

Children Act 1989
London: HMSO, 1989

Crime and Disorder Act 1998
London: The Stationery Office, 1998

Department for Education & Employment, Department of Health
Consultation paper on the regulation of early education and day care
London: Department for Education & Employment, 1998

Department of the Environment, Transport and the Regions
Modern local government: in touch with the people
London: The Stationery Office, 1998 (Cm. 4014)

Department of Health
Adoption: Achieving the right balance
London: Department of Health, 1998
(Local Authority Circular; LAC(98)20).

Department of Health Children's Services Branch
*Working together to safeguard children: new government proposals
for inter-agency co-operation: consultation paper*
London: Department of Health, 1998

Department of Health, Department for Education & Employment,
Home Office, Welsh Office
Establishing youth offending teams
London: Department of Health, 1998
(Health Service Circular: HSC 1998/090)

Department of Health, Department of the Environment
Housing and community care: establishing a strategic framework
London: Department of Health, 1997

Department of Health, Government Statistical Service
*Children looked after by local authorities, year ending 31 March 1997,
England*
London: Department of Health, 1998

Department of Health
*Modernising health and social services: National priorities guidance
1999/00 – 2001/02*
London: Department of Health, 1998

Department of Health
Our healthier nation: a contract for health
London: The Stationery Office, 1998 (Cm. 3852)

Department of Health Social Services Inspectorate
*Social services facing the future: the seventh annual report of the Chief
Inspector, Social Services Inspectorate, 1997/98*
London: The Stationery Office, 1998

Department of Health
The new NHS: modern, dependable
London: The Stationery Office, 1997 (Cm. 3807)

Department of Health
The safety of children and young people in the public care
London: Department of Health, 1997. (Chief Inspector; CI(97)29)

Department of Health
The safety of children and young people in the public care
London: Department of Health, 1997. (Chief Inspector; CI(97)10)

Goss S
A framework for housing with support: a tool to describe,
evaluate and continuously improve services
London: National Housing Federation, 1998

HM Treasury & Cabinet Office
Modern public services for Britain: investing in reform
London: The Stationery Office, 1998. (Cm. 4011)

Hoare L, Stranger C, Adams K, et al
Someone else's children: inspections of planning and decision making for
children looked after and the safety of children looked after
London: Department of Health, 1998. (Social Services Inspectorate
report; no. 415)

Home Office
Compact on relations between Government and the voluntary
and community sector in England
London: The Stationery Office, 1998. (Cm. 4100)

Home Office, Department of Health, Department of
Education and Science, Welsh Office
Working together under the Children Act 1989: a guide to arrangements
for inter-agency co-operation for the protection of children from abuse
London: HMSO, 1991

House of Commons Health Committee
Children looked after by local authorities: second report from
the Health Committee. Session 1997 – 98
London: The Stationery Office, 1998
Chairman: David Hinchliffe. (HC 319; vol II)

Jones A, Clark PA, Pont C, Department of Health Social Services
Inspectorate
Messages from inspection: child protection inspection 1992 – 1996
London: Department of Health, 1997

Local Authority Social Services Act 1970
London: HMSO, 1970

Means R, Benton M, Harrison L
*Making partnerships work in community care: a guide for practitioners
in housing, health and social services*
Bristol: University of Bristol Policy Press, 1997

Mental Health Act 1983
London: HMSO, 1983

Patel C, Haskins C, Better Regulation Task Force, Central Office
of Information
Long-term Care
London: Central Office of Information, 1998

Registered Homes Act 1984
London: HMSO, 1984

Social Exclusion Unit
Bringing Britain together: a national strategy for neighbourhood renewal
London: The Stationery Office, 1998. (Cm. 4045)

Home Office
Supporting families
London: The Stationery Office, 1998

The Labour Party
New Labour because Britain deserves better
London: The Labour Party, 1997

Utting W, Baines C, Stuart M, et al
*People like us: the report of the review of the safeguards for children
living away from home*
London: The Stationery Office, 1997

To obtain a copy of the draft regulatory impact appraisal for the proposals in Chapter 4, write to:

Barbara Erne, Room 625, Wellington House, 133-155 Waterloo Road, London SE1 8UG

or you can get it on the Internet at:

http://www.doh.gov.uk/dhhome.htm

This White Paper is also available on the Internet at:

http://www.official-documents.co.uk/document/cm41/4169/4169.htm

Printed in the UK for The Stationery Office Limited on behalf of the
Controller of Her Majesty's Stationery Office
Dd 5068487. 11/98. 61743. Job No 66775.